WHAT PEOPLE ARE SAYING ABOUT "NAME THAT PET!"

Name That Pet!

A Practical Guide to Naming Your Dog, Cat and Other Household Pets

Naomi Jones

Cousin Alice's Press

Los Angeles, California

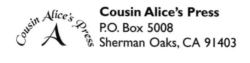

Cousin Alice's Press
P.O. Box 5008
Sherman Oaks, CA 91403

Copyright © 2004 by Naomi Jones

ISBN: 0-9719786-3-8

Cover graphics and book design by Syzygy Design Group, Inc.
Cover illustration by Susan Gal Illustration
Interior illustrations by Tanya Stewart Illustration

Printed by United Graphics Inc.
Printed in the United States of America

First Printing: October 2004

Publisher's Cataloging-in-Publication

Jones, Naomi
    Name that pet! / Naomi Jones. -- 1st ed.
    p. cm.
    ISBN 0-9719786-3-8

    1. Pets--Names.   I. Title.
SF411.3.L54 2004   929.9'7
                                     QBI02-200487

10 9 8 7 6 5 4 3 2 1

ACKNOWLEDGEMENTS

This book was a labor of love, and without the ongoing support of my family and friends, could not have come to fruition. I very much want to thank those individuals whose tireless devotion and commitment has made its publication possible.

Thank you Suzie McKig of Syzygy Design Group for your graphics expertise and ongoing support; Collete Ostrye whose superior Librarian skills created a solid foundation to work from; Laurie Welch for her incisive research and genuine enthusiasm for this project; Goldie Paquet for her eagle-eye for detail; Tanya Stewart whose exquisite illustrations tell the story, and Pamela Terry of Opus I Design; her finishing touches and keen publishing expertise enabled me to move forward.

A special thanks to my family of aunts, uncles, cousins and friends whose lifetime of unconditional support and love, have kept me moving forward.

And finally, to my mother, who proclaimed my talent for music and art, before I even had any.

This book is dedicated to the loving memory of my father; Aunt Tillie; Eddie; Grandma Anna; Christopher; Michael, and Cousin Alice. You live in my heart.

Name That Pet!

A Practical Guide to Naming Your
Dog, Cat and Other Household Pets

Table of Contents

CHAPTER 1

INTRODUCTION

Congratulations, new pet owner! You have acquired the newest member of your family. He is loving, soft and playful, or scaly and creepy-crawly. He could either be small or large, thick furred or hairless, exuberant or low-key. What he needs is a name that fully describes his personality, his uniqueness. A name he will respond to happily, though he will never get a complex from an unflattering name!

Here in these pages exist over 3000 choices that the whole family can have fun with. Methodically go through each name and take a moment to conjure up an image. If the shoe fits...

If your children have a favorite cartoon or storybook character, they will have a lot of fun choosing from these chapters. Do not be surprised to see many that trigger fond memories from your own childhood. Or, if you are a family of music aficionados, there are many musicians that you may want your pet to honor. The kids may love *Beyoncé* or *Sisqo,* though *Wolfgang* or *Amadeus* may reflect your own classical preference.

Our culture has produced so many T.V. and movie stars or memorable characters. *Benji* is just one of many endearing wonder dogs that have come from these mediums. How about calling him *Doogie Bowser*, or *Alfalfa* or *Spanky* from "Our Gang"? Who does he remind you of?

If your pet is a northern breed, that chapter will provide names that are more indigenous to a colder climate such as *Aspen* or *Grizzly*. Perhaps, if you have a purebred from a particular country or region, see the section on "Ethnic Origins." Watch the amusing looks you get when introducing your English Bullmastiff, *Big Ben*. If you own a Russian wolfhound and are a Sacramento Kings fan, then *Vlade* could not be more perfect. You may even select a name based on your own culture.

Having acquired two lovebirds, or siblings from the same litter, the chapter "Dynamic Duos" will list many famous pairs, both male and female, or a combination of each. Or, if his color is outstanding: a beautiful Irish Setter, Chocolate Lab, or Harlequin Great Dane, try *Scarlet, Kahlúa* or *Oreo*. The color section will provide names that will make him stand out even more.

If you have a new exotic Himalayan or Abyssinian feline friend, see the chapter on "Cats."

Do you have a wicked sense of humor? Naming your toy poodle *Hannibal the Cannibal* will surely raise some eyebrows. But if it's your pet that has a wit of his own, then review the "Funsters" chapter. Here you'll find names like *Hijinks* or *Gilligan* that capture his whimsical nature. Also found here are some of the world's renowned comedians.

INTRODUCTION

Besides all the people you might love, do not forget those we love to hate. In "Antiheroes" there are infamous villains and the like. Although historically there are the more noteworthy pets, perhaps your animal companion would like to be named after a First Family pet, as described in "Presidents' Pets." Just be sure his name does not sound similar to an obedience command.

For everyone's tastes, from sports to music, there is a name for any pet. Be creative and take your time. Remember, you will be referring to this name each day and forever. Let your imagination run wild; the possibilities are endless. Have fun!

CHAPTER 2

FAMOUS PETS

ARGO-ARGUS. Ulysses' hunting dog was the only creature to recognize the Greek hero when he returned home disguised as a beggar after 20 years of adventure.

BALTO. An Eskimo dog led a dog team that carried diphtheria serum 650 miles (1050 kilometers) through an Alaskan blizzard from Nenana to Nome in 1925.

BARRY. A St. Bernard rescued 40 persons lost in the snows of Switzerland's St. Bernard Pass about 1800.

CAESAR. A terrier, which was the pet of King Edward VII of Great Britain. He walked ahead of Kings and Princes in his master's funeral procession in 1910.

CERBERUS. The three-headed dog of Greek Mythology guarded the gates to the underworld.

IGLOO. A fox terrier was the special pet of Admiral Richard E. Byrd. He flew with Bryd in flights over the North and South Poles.

LAIKA. The world's first space traveler, Laika rode aboard Sputnik II, an artificial earth satellite on November 3, 1957.

PUNXSUTAWNEY PHIL Punxsutawney, Pennsylvania, home of the world-famous weather forecasting groundhog, Punxsutawney Phil. The prediction is, if he sees his shadow on February 2nd, there will be six more weeks of winter.

CHAPTER 3

PRESIDENT'S PETS

GEORGE WASHINGTON. (1789-1797). Hounds: Mopsey, Taster, Cloe, Tipler, Forester, Captain, Lady, Rover, Vulcan, Sweetlips and Searcher.

ABRAHAM LINCOLN. (1861-1865). Mutts: Fido and Jip.

ULYSSES S. GRANT. (1869-1877). Newfoundland: Faithful.

JAMES A. GARFIELD. (1831-1881). Mixed breeds: Veto.

THEODORE ROOSEVELT. (1901-1909). Bull Terrier: Pete. Chesapeake Bay Retriever: Sailor Boy. Mutt: Skip. Spaniel: Manchu. Terrier: Jack.

WARREN G. HARDING. (1921-1923). Airedale: Laddieboy.

CALVIN COOLIDGE. (1923-1929). Airedale: Paul Pry. Bird Dog: Palo Alto. Brown Collie: Boston Beans. Chow: Blackberry. Police Dog: King Cole. Shetland Sheepdog: Calamity Jane. Terrier: Peter Pan. White Collies: Rob Roy and Prudence Prim. Yellow Collie: Bessie.

HERBERT HOOVER. (1929-1933). Elkhound: Weejie. Eskimo Dog: Yukon. Fox Terriers: Big Ben and Sonnie. Police Dog: King Tut and Pat. Scottish Terrier Collie: Glen. Setter: Eaglehurst Gilette. Wolfhound: Patrick.

FRANKLIN D. ROOSEVELT. (1933-1945). English Sheepdog: Tiny. German Shepherd: Major. Great Dane: President. Mastiff: Blaze. Setter: Wink. Scottish Terriers: Meggie, Llewellyn and Fala.

HARRY S. TRUMAN. (1945-1953). Mutt: Feller, "The Unwanted Dog." Margaret Truman's Irish Setter: Mike.

DWIGHT D. EISENHOWER. (1953-1961). Scottie: Spunky. Weimaraner: Heide.

JOHN F. KENNEDY. (1961-1963). Mutt: Pushinka and Wolf. Poodle: Vicky. Shepherd: Clipper. Spaniel: Shannon. Terriers: Charley and Pasha. Others: Butterfly, White Tips, Blackie and Streaker.

LYNDON B. JOHNSON. (1963-1969). Beagles: Him and Her.

RICHARD M. NIXON. (1969-1974). Cocker Spaniel: Checkers. Irish Setter: King Timahoe.

GERALD FORD. (1974-1977). Retriever: Liberty.

RONALD REAGAN. (1981-1989). Beauvier de Flanders: Lucky. Doberman/Mix: Freebo. Golden Retriever: Victory. Husky: Taca.

GEORGE BUSH. (1989-1993). Springer Spaniel: Millie.

BILL CLINTON. (1993-2001). Cat: Socks, daughter Chelsea's black and white tabby. When Clinton left office, Socks moved in with his secretary, Betty Curry. Beloved Chocolate Lab: Buddy. (1997-2001).

GEORGE W. BUSH. (2001-). English Springer Spaniel: Spot. Scottish Terrier: Barney. Cat: India.

CHAPTER 4

75 MOST POPULAR DOG NAMES

MALE	Buster	Max	Sam
Bandit	Charlie	Otto	Shep
Baron	Conan	Prince	Tiger
Beau	Duke	Rambo	Winston
Benji	Jake	Rocky	Woody
Brutus	King	Rommel	Zack
Buck	Major	Rudy	

UNISEX	Brandy	Lucky	Spot
Baby	Buddy	Misty	T.J.
Bear	Casey	Puppy	Whiskers
Blackie	Cody	Rusty	
Blue	D.O.G.	Shadow	

FEMALE	Ginger	Maxi	Sunny
Abby	Gypsy	Molly	Sunshine
Amber	Heide	Nikki	Taffy
Ashley	Honey	Princess	Tanya
Buffy	Katie	Roxie	Tasha
Chelsea	Kayla	Samantha	Trixie
Coco	Lady	Sasha	
Dusty	Maggie	Shana	
Fluffy	Mandy	Shasta	

CHAPTER 5

DYNAMIC DUOS

Should you acquire two siblings from the same litter or the like, the following are lists of couples, so that you can pair their names. Do create your own fun combinations as well.

FAMOUS PAIRS

MALE & FEMALE

Barbie & Ken

Beldar and Prymaat

Bonnie & Clyde

Boris & Natasha

Count & Countess

Dagwood & Blondie

Dude & Dudette

Frankie & Johnnie

Fred & Ethel

Fred & Ginger

Fred & Wilma

Hansel & Gretel

Jack & Jill

Lucy & Ricky

Mickey & Minnie

Mork & Mindy

Natasha & Boris

Ozzie & Harriet

Peaches & Herb

Pebbles & Bam Bam

Popeye & Olive Oyl

Porgy & Bess

Raggedy Ann
& Raggedy Andy

Romeo & Juliet

Samson & Delilah

Scarlett & Rhett

Sonny & Cher

Sugar & Spice

MALE & MALE

Abbott & Costello

Amos & Andy

Barnum & Bailey

Batman & Robin

Beanie & Cecil

Bert & Ernie

Bill & Ted

Buzz & Woody

Calvin & Hobbes

Charlie & Bronson

Cheech & Chong

Crockett & Tubbs

Dr. Jekyl & Mr. Hyde

Felix & Oscar

Gibson & Glover

Hans & Franz

Heckle & Jeckle

NAME THAT PET!

Homer & Bart

Ike & Mike

Jake and Elwood

Laurel & Hardy

Lenny & Squiggy

Lone Ranger
& Tonto

Kenan & Kel

Mr. Moose &
Bunny Rabbit

Mutt & Jeff

Orville & Wilbur

Ren & Stimpy

Rocky
& Bullwinkle

Sherlock Holmes
& Dr. Watson

Sherman & Peabody

Starsky & Hutch

Thunderbolt

& Lightfoot

Tom & Jerry

Tweedle Dee
& Tweedle Dum

Wayne & Garth

Yogi & Boo Boo

FEMALE & FEMALE

Cagney & Lacey

Isis & Electra

Salt & Pepa

Thelma & Louise

Xena & Gabrielle

UNISEX DUOS

Buttons & Bows

Catbert & Dogbert

Chip & Dale

Ebony & Ivory

Frick & Frack

Humpty & Dumpty

Nip & Tuck

Sugar & Spice

Thunder &
Lightning

Yin & Yang

CHAPTER 6

"SIZEABLE" NAMES

SMALL PETS

Bitsey	Little Big Man	Pipsqueak	Tadpole
Bullet	Little Boy Blue	Pixie	Teacup
Buttercup	Little Dipper	Pookie	Teeny Weenie
Cricket	Little Girl	Poptart	Tic Tac
Cupcake	Little Orphan	Poquito	Tidbit
Elf	Annie	Pygmy	Tinkerbell
Flea	Midget	Ratdog	Toy Toy
Gizmo	Mini Me	Runt	Trifle
Gnome	Muffin	Shrimp	Trinket
Half-pint	Munchkin	Skittles	Troll
Inch	Negrita	Smidgen	Twiggy
Itsy Bitsy	Peanut	Sprout	Weasel
Lil' Abner	Peapod	Squint	Wienie
Lil' Guy	Pee Wee	Squirt	
Lil' Bit	Piglet	Stumpy	

NAME THAT PET!

LARGE PETS

Ali	Gargantua	Magnum	Tiny
Amazon	Gentle Ben	Mama Cass	Titan
Ape Man	Gigantor	Mammoth	Titanic
Arnold	Gnarly	Marmaduke	Tornado
Atlas	Godzilla	Moby Dick	Toro
Beefy	Gordo	Moose	
Big Bopper	Heavy D.	Mr. Big	
Big Dipper	Hercules	Mr. Muscles	
Big Foot	Holmes	Orca	
Bigger	Hulk Hogan	Rin Tin Tin	
Biggs	Juggernaut	Samson	
Blimpie	Jumbo	Sasquatch	
Brutus	Kareem	Shamu	
Bull	King	Sumo	
Cujo	Kong	Tsunami	
Dr. J	Kubiak	Tank	
Fatboy Slim	Lummox	Tarzan	
Fatso	Magilla Gorilla	Tempest	

CHAPTER 7

MUSIC

MUSICIANS

AAHLIYAH. Aahliyah Houghton (1979-2001). This singer had recorded three albums; the self-titled "Aahliyah" issued just one month before she died in a plane crash in the Bahamas. In 2002 she received 2 posthumous American Music Awards.

AMADEUS. Middle name of the composer Wolfgang Amadeus Mozart. See "Mozart."

ANASTACIA. (1973-). Chicago born and New York raised singer, whose first album is entitled "Not that Kind."

ANGUS. Angus Young, a guitarist for the heavy metal Australian band "AC/DC."

ARETHA. Aretha Franklin (1941-). The "Queen of Soul" started singing in her father's church. She is most recognized for her hit "R-E-S-P-E-C-T."

ARLO. Arlo Guthrie (1947-). Folk singer and composer; Arlo is known for his song "Alice's Restaurant."

AXL. Axl Rose. Bill Bailey (1962-). Lead singer for the heavy metal "do it to excess," rock group "Guns 'n Roses."

B.B. KING. Riley B. "BB" King (1925-). B.B. is known as "King of the Blues." With albums, awards, and nightclubs, B.B. is a crowd pleaser.

BACH. Johann Sebastian Bach (1685-1750). German organist and composer of instrumental and vocal music.

BEASTIE BOY. Rap group known for excess. Led by the singer Adam Yauch, who helped coin the 1980's youth call "You gotta fight for the right to party."

BEETHOVEN. Ludwig van Beethoven (1770-1827). German composer, although deaf, composed the world's greatest symphonies.

BEE GEE. A Bee Gee is a Gibb brother in the "Bee Gees." Most recognized for their double album "Saturday Night Fever."

BEYONCÉ. (1981-). Beyoncé Knowles, formerly of Destiny's Child is riding high on the success of her first album, Grammy winning, "Dangerously in Love" (2003).

BLACKSTREET. Highly regarded young, urban R&B band. First hit single "Before I Let You Go" (1994).

BLONDIE. This punk-rock group was formed by bleached blonde Deborah Harry and Chris Stein. "Heart of Glass" (1980).

BO DIDDLEY. Elias McDaniel. As a rhythm and blues artist, his first single "Bo Diddley" was a hit in 1955.

BON JOVI. Jon Bon Jovi. Born John Bongiovi (1962-). As the leader of a pop-metal band, his music addresses middle-class teen sensibilities. Hits include "Living on a Prayer" and "It's My Life."

BONE THUGS AND HARMONY. Grammy Award Winning Quartet from Cleveland, OH whose M-O is "Reality Rap."

BONO. Bono Hewson (1960-). Vocalist for Irish rock band "U2." Bono is also instrumental in bringing attention to world debt.

THE BOSS. Nickname for Bruce Springsteen. See "Bruce."

BOWIE. Born David Jones (1947-). David Bowie is most known for his flamboyant characterizations as well as his unabashed rock-n-roll such as "Ch-ch-ch-changes."

BRAHMS. Johannes Brahms (1833-1897). German composer of many songs and arrangements of German folk songs like Brahms' "Lullaby."

BRUCE. Bruce Springsteen (1949-). Jersey rocker best known for his blue collar rock-n-roll. He and "The E Street Band" tear up the stage with their 4 hour, high voltage, live shows with crowd-pleasers such as "Born to Run" and "Rosalita."

BUSTER POINDEXTER. David Johansen (1950-). Lead singer for the glam-rock band "The New York Dolls." He later became Buster Poindexter, the lounge singer with the hit "Hot Hot Hot."

CARNIE. Carnie Wilson (1969-). Vocalist with pop music group "Wilson Phillips" is the daughter of "Beach Boys" Brian Wilson.

CHAKA. Chaka Khan, lead singer for soul/funk band "Rufus." Hits include "Tell Me Something Good" and "You've Got the Love."

CHARO. (1942-). Maria Rosario Pilar Martinez Molina Baeza. Blonde, Spanish spitfire, Charo is the "Cuchi Cuchi" girl. Although known for her sexy flamboyance and comedy, she is a gifted classical guitarist and singer.

CHOPIN. Frederic Chopin (1810-1849). Polish composer, who lived most of his life in Paris.

CHYNNA. Chynna Phillips (1968-). Vocalist with pop music group "Wilson Phillips," is the daughter of former members of "Mamas and Papas" John and Michelle Phillips.

CLARENCE. Clarence Clemons (1942-). Super saxophonist with Bruce Springsteen's "E Street Band" and his solo band "The Red Band Rockers."

DEVO. Short for Devo-lution. Most famous for their frenetic hit "Whip It" (1980).

DESTINY'S CHILD. Female R&B group, whose members include, Beyoncé Knowles, Kelly Rowland and Michelle Williams. Their breakout album "The Writing's on the Wall" sold 10 million copies worldwide.

DIDO. Dido Armstrong (1971-). English pop star whose hit "Here with Me" is off of her breakout album, now platinum "No Angel" (1999). See also "Mythology."

DION. Dion Dimucci (1939-). "Dion and the Belmonts" established themselves with their first single "I Wonder Why" (1958). Later, "Abraham, Martin and John" became a classic.

DIZZY. John Birks "Dizzy Gillespie" (1917-1993). Jazz trumpeter and bandleader, who with Charlie Parker pioneered Be-Bop.

DOC. Carl Hilding "Doc" Severinson (1927-). Trumpet player; for 20 years, the band leader for "The Tonight Show."

DOLLY. Dolly Parton (1946-). This irrepressible country-western singer is known for her flamboyant style, supple voice and prolific songwriting skills. Best known for "9-5" and "Islands in the Stream" with Kenny Rogers.

DONOVAN. Donovan Leitch (1946-). This English Bob Dylan is most famous for hits "Mellow Yellow" and "Sunshine Superman."

DOOBIE. A doobie is an unrelated member of the rock band "Doobie Brothers." Hits include "China Grove" and "Rocking Down the Highway."

DR. DRE. Andre Young (1965-). Gansta rap pioneer, with breakout album "The Chronic."

DWEEZIL. Eldest son of pop/rock musician Frank Zappa, Dweezil is a guitarist and rock singer.

DYLAN. Robert Allen Zimmerman (1941-). This folk singer/poet is often recognized as an early influence to many musicians. Hits include "Blowin' in the Wind" and "Hurricane."

EARTHA KITT. Eartha Mae Kitt (1928-). Dancer/actress was a soloist with the "Katherine Dunham Dance Group" (1948).

ELFMAN. Danny Elfman is a member of the band "Oingo Boingo" and composer of scores for the films "Batman" and "Dick Tracy."

EMINEM. Marshall Mathers III (1972-). Controversial rapper/actor, whose alter ego, Slim Shady is revered by youth, reviled by parents. Debuted in film "8 Mile" (2002).

ENGLEBERT. Arnold Gerry Dorsey (1936). Englebert's hits include "Release Me" and "After the Lovin'."

EUBIE. James Hubert "Eubie" Blake. (1883-1983). Noted for his ragtime, stride piano.

FABIAN. Fabiano Forte (1943-). Singer whose hits include "Lillie Lou" and "Turn Me Loose."

FAITH HILL. Audrey Faith Perry (1967-). Country music singer. A triple Grammy winner in 2001 for the album and single "Breathe."

FATBOY SLIM. Norman Cook (1963-). Raucous blend of house, acid, funk, hip-hop, electro, and techno has added to his already formidable reputation as one of the foremost all-around producers on the U.K. club scene.

FELIX CAVALIERE. (1944-). Lead Singer of the rock group "The Little Rascals." Best known for their hit "Good Lovin" (1965).

FREDDIE MERCURY. (1946-1991). Androgynous vocalist of British rock band "Queen." Best known for his vocal theatrics on the hit "Bohemian Rhapsody."

FRESH PRINCE. "Will" Willard Smith (1969-). Singer/actor was half of the rap duo "D.J. Jazzy Jeff and The Fresh Prince." First rap group to ever win a Grammy in the rap category.

FUGEES. Rap crossover band. Two members of the group, Wyclef Jean and his cousin Pras, born in Haiti, prompted the name, Fugee that is short for "refugee".

GARTH. Troyal Garth Brooks (1962-). An award winning country music vocalist, he is the biggest selling solo artist of all time, selling over 100 million albums.

GERSHWIN. George Gershwin (1898-1937). American composer who combined elements of classical music with elements of popular music from "Rhapsody in Blue" to "Porgy and Bess."

HAMMER. M.C. Hammer. Stanley Kirk Burrell (1963-). First rap artist to achieve crossover popularity with his frenetic hit "You Can't Touch This."

HEAVY D. Dwight Meyers. (1967-). Jamaican born, but raised in the Bronx, this rhythm and blues rapper with 3 platinum records is "Livin' Large" as a singer and actor.

HOLLY. Charles Harden "Buddy" Holley (1936-1959). With the band "The Crickets" who recorded the hits "Maybe Baby" and "Peggy Sue."

ICE CUBE. O'Shea Jackson (1969-). This rapper/actor is a former member and songwriter for rap group N.W.A. Went on to star in ground breaking film "Boyz in the Hood" (1991).

ICE T. Tracy Morrow (1959-). Rap artist/actor. Raps about inner city street life. He's also been successful in film and on T.V.

IKE. Ike Turner (1931-). See "Tina Turner."

J.LO. Jennifer Lopez (1970-). Singer, dancer, actress. This Bronx beauty has the distinction of having the first #1 album and movie in the same week.

J.T. James Taylor (1948-). This Grammy winner is a singer, songwriter, and guitarist. As a soft rock balladeer, his hits include "Fire and Rain" and "Sweet Baby James."

JAGGER. Mick Jagger (1941-). The lead singer of the most enduring rock-n-roll band "The Rolling Stones," whose hits include "Satisfaction" and "Brown Sugar."

JAZZY JEFF. D.J. Jazzy Jeff. Jeffrey Townes (1965-). See "Fresh Prince."

JEWEL. Jewel Kilcher (1974-). Angelic voiced singer from Alaska with breakout album "Pieces of You" (1995).

JOPLIN. Janis Joplin (1943-1970). In 1966, she became lead vocalist with the band, Big Brother and the Holding Company; Kosmic Blues Band (1968-1970), & The Full Tilt Boogie Band. This bluesy-rocker is best known for her hits "Me and Bobby McGee" and "Cry Baby."

JOPLIN. Scott Joplin 1868-1917). The "King of Ragtime" is best known for this work "The Maple Leaf Rag."

K.D. Katherine Dawn "k.d." Lang (1961-). Originally a country music singer, her release in 1992 of "Ingénue" reflected a new direction for this Grammy award-winning singer.

KOOL MOE DEE. Mohandas Dewese (1963-). In 1989, his gold album "Knowledge is King" affirmed hip-hop's prominence into the mainstream, as he performed at the Grammy Awards, becoming the first rapper to do so.

L.L. COOL J. James Todd (Ladies Love Cool James) Smith (1968-). Rap artist/actor/writer who had his first single "I Can't Live Without My Radio" (1985) at just 18 years old. He had his own T.V. sitcom "In the House" and starred in films like "Rollerball" (2002).

LIBERACE. Wladziu Valentino Liberace (1919-1987). Flamboyant pianist and entertainer, who lived an ostentatious lifestyle.

LIONEL. Lionel Hampton (1908-). Started out as a drummer, became proficient as a jazz vibraphonist, and formed his first big band in 1932.

LOLLAPALOOZA. Heavy metal rock extravaganza tour.

MACY GRAY. (1970-). Grammy award winner was born Natalie McIntyre. Macy's voice has been compared to Billie Holiday and Tina Turner. Her breakout album "On How Life Is" (1999) includes the hits "I Try" and "Caligula."

MADONNA. Madonna Louise Veronica Ciccone (1958-). Singer/ actress, famous for reinventing her image and for her provocative style. Her hits include "Material Girl," "Ray of Light" and "Music."

MAMA CASS. Cass Elliott (1943-1974). Mama Cass provided vocals in the folk rock group "The Mamas and the Papas" with their first recording in 1966 "California Dreamin'."

MARIAH. Mariah Carey (1970-). Grammy award winning pop vocalist with an 8-octave vocal range. Her 1990 debut album featured her hit single "Vision of Love." Other hits include "Butterfly" and "Emotions."

MARLEY, BOB. Robert Nesta Marley (1945-1981). Bob Marley and the Wailers are known worldwide for their special brand of reggae. Remembered for hits like "No Woman No Cry" and "Zimbabwe," Bob Marley's death in 1981 has not stopped the love and recognition from his fans.

MELBA. Melba Moore (1947-). Songstress has appeared in the musical "Hair" and won a Tony award for "Purlie."

METALLICA. Heavy metal rock band. They won their fifth Grammy in 2001 for their album "Whiskey in the Jar."

MILES. Miles Davis (1926-1991). One of the great jazz musicians, he played the trumpet and collaborated with other jazz greats.

MOBY. Richard Melville Hall (1965-). Moby is a relative of the famous whale story author. He is eclectic in his musical style, as evident in the album "Play" (1999).

MOON UNIT. (1967-). Daughter of pop/rock musician Frank Zappa. Hit single was "Valley Girl."

MOZART. Wolfgang Amadeus Mozart (1756-1791). Austrian composer. Child prodigy who, through the years, wrote at least 600 compositions.

MUDDY WATERS. McKinley Morgan Field (1915-1983). As one of the great blues singers, he influenced many soul and rock musicians.

NELLY. Nelly Furtado (1978-). Portuguese-Canadian singer-songwriter whose debut album "Whoa Nelly!" Spawned the hits "Turn Off the Light" and "I'm Like a Bird," for which she won the 2002 Grammy for Best Female Pop Vocal Performance.

NELSON. Eric "Rick" Hilliard Nelson (1940-1985). Worked with his T.V. family "Ozzie and Harriet." Hits include "I'm Walkin'" (1957) and "Garden Party" (1972). Twin sons, Gunner & Matthew have their own rock band "Nelson."

PAVAROTTI. Luciano Pavarotti (1935-). Italian tenor has sung opera on the world's great stages.

P-DIDDY. See "Puffy Daddy."

PEABO. Robert Peabo Bryson (1951-). Rhythm and blues singer, recorded top 40 hit with Roberta Flack "Tonight, I Celebrate My Love" (1983).

PEACHES AND HERB. Francine Hurd (1947-). Herb Feemster (1942-). A singing duo with the R&B hit "Reunited" (1978).

PETULA. Petula Clark (1932-). Pop vocalist of the 60's. Her big hit was "Downtown" (1964).

PHOEBE. Phoebe Snow (1952-). Her unique style combines blues, jazz and folk. Most known for her single "Poetry Man."

POCO. Group formed in 1968 by Richie Furay (from "Buffalo Springfield") and Jim Messina (later "Loggins and Messina").

PORTER. Cole Porter (1892-1964). Composer of popular music. Wrote musicals and is known for such Frank Sinatra classics as "I Get a Kick Out of You" and "I've Got You Under My Skin."

POSH. Victoria "Posh Spice" Adams Beckham (1974). See "Spice Girls."

PRINCE. Prince Rogers Nelson (1958-). The "Purple One" is a critically acclaimed musician, singer and songwriter. He reached superstar status with the release of "Purple Rain" (1984).

PUCCINI. Giacomo Puccini (1858-1924). Italian composer whose works include "Madame Butterfly" and "La Boheme."

PUFF DADDY. Sean "Puffy" Combs (1970-). Rapper/producer created a multi-million dollar industry around Bad Boy Entertainment. The biggest hip-hop impresario of the mid-'90s has also branched out in fashion merchandising and acting.

QUEEN LATIFAH. Dana Owens (1970-). A socially conscious female rapper, actress and talk show host.

RASCAL. See "Felix Cavalieri."

REBA. Reba McEntire (1954-). Country music vocalist and Grammy winner, now star of her own T.V. show "Reba" (2001-).

RINGO. Richard Starkey (1948-). Drummer of the rock group "The Beatles." Had solo hit "You're Sixteen" and travels with his "All Star Band."

ROXETTE. Name of the Swedish rock duo (Marie Fredriksson and Per Gessle) with the hit song "Almost Unreal" from the film "Super Mario Brothers."

RUFUS. See "Chaka Kahn."

SALT-N-PEPA. A female rap group with the 1987 gold hit "Push It." Trio includes Cheryl James, Sandy Denton and Dee Roper.

SATCHMO. Louis Armstrong (1900-1971). The great jazz trumpeter and entertainer.

SAXON. A heavy metal band from the United Kingdom.

SCHUBERT. Franz Peter Schubert (1797-1828). Austrian composer known for his lieder compositions (over 600 songs).

SHAGGY. Orville Richard Burrell (1968-). His worldwide hit, a cover of "Oh Carolina" put New York Reggae on the map. He describes his style of music as "dog-a-muffin" which are elements of jazz and raggamuffin.

SHEENA. Shirley Orr Easton (1959-). Scottish singer's first single was "Morning Train" (1980). Recorded the theme from the 1981 James Bond film "For Your Eyes Only."

SISQO. Mark Andrews (1978-). Colorful Baltimore rapper/actor, famous for the hit "The Thong Song."

SLASH. Saul Hudson (1965-). Lead guitarist for the heavy metal band Guns n' Roses.

SLICK. Grace Slick (1943-). Vocalist with the San Francisco/ Haight Ashbury based 60's rock group Jefferson Airplane and later Starship.

SMOKEY. William "Smokey" Robinson (1940-). Grammy winning singer was with "Smokey Robinson and the Miracles" from 1957 to 1972. Hits include "Tracks of My Tears" and "Tears of a Clown."

SPICE GIRL. The Spice Girls, an English girl group, expressed their "Girl Power" philosophy. Their first single in 1996 was "Wannabe."

SPINNER. The Spinners were a Detroit R&B group with their hit songs "I'll be Around" and "Could it be I'm Fallin' in Love?"

SPIRIT. Rock group formed in 1965 in Los Angeles. Best known single "Stuck in the Middle With You."

SQUEEZE. London-based band, which came to prominence in the late 1970's, during the New Wave movement.

SQUIER. Rocker Billy Squier's most notable work is "All Night Long" (1984).

STING. Gordon Matthew Sumner (1951-). Bass guitar player and vocalist for the reggae-influenced rock group "The Police." Sting went on to a successful solo career whose hits include "If You Love Somebody Set The Free" and "If I Ever Lose My Faith in You".

STRAUSS. Johann, father (1804-1849) and son (1825-1899). Violinist, conductor and composer of waltzes.

STRAVINSKY. Igor Stravinsky (1882-1971). Composer of ballets "The Fire Bird" and "Petrushka."

STRAY CATS. Rockabilly band playing 50's style rock with the hit "Rock This Town."

SURVIVOR. Rock band with the hit single "Eye of the Tiger" in 1982.

THELONIOUS SPHERE MONK. (1917-1982). Jazz musician; he helped to birth "Bebop." He played with the Dizzy Gillespie Orchestra in 1940's, but by the '50's he was recognized for his own contributions to jazz.

TINA. Annie Mae "Tina" Bullock (1939-). Married Ike Turner and formed "The Ike and Tina Turner Revue." Hits include "Proud Mary" and solo hit "What's Love Got to do With It?"

TITO. Tito Puente. (1923-2000). Grammy award winning Latin jazz musician has recorded over 100 albums.

U2. Irish rock band whose lyrics are of a socially and politically conscious nature. Hits include "Sunday, Bloody Sunday" and "In The Name of Love."

VANILLA ICE. Robert Van Winkle (1968-). Miami rapper whose first single was "Ice Ice Baby."

WAYLON. Waylon Arnold Jennings (1937-2002). "Outlaw" country rock musician, composer and actor. Teamed up with Kris Kristofferson, Johnny Cash and Willie Nelson 1985 to form the supergroup "The Highwaymen."

WEEZER. Post-grunge alternative rock band, whose music is infused with a quirky sense of humor and endearing awkwardness that made songs like "Undone (The Sweater Song)" and "Buddy Holly" (1994, 1995), hits.

WILLIE. Willie Nelson (1933-). Legendary country rock musician who is best known for the hit single "On the Road Again" and the album "The Redheaded Stranger."

WOODSTOCK. (1969). Outdoor music festival. Featured top artists like: Janis Joplin. Jimi Hendrix, Jefferson Airplane, Joan Baez. Thirty years later another festival was organized, which included Metallica Counting Crows and Jewel, among others.

XAVIER. Xavier Cugat (1900-1990). As a bandleader in New York City, he was known as the "Rumba King."

YANNI. Yanni Chryssomalis. (1954-). A musician with perfect pitch, he was born in Kalamata, Greece and came to the US in 1972. Known for his musical extravaganzas at the Acropolis and Taj Mahal, he is the Greek God of New Age music.

YOKO. Yoko Ono. (1933-). A 1960's avant-artist in New York. She met Beatle John Lennon at one of her art exhibits and married him in 1969.

YOUNG MC. Marvin Young (1967-). Socially conscious rapper recorded the hit "Bust-A-Move" (1989).

YO-YO MA. (1955-). Premiere classical cellist, who is also known for his performance on the sound track for the film "Crouching Tiger, Hidden Dragon" (2000).

ZAPPA. Frank Zappa (1940-1993). Unconventional rocker with his band "Mothers of Invention" recorded cult hits like "Dental Floss."

MUSICAL CHARACTERS

ARROW. "Me and My Arrow," a song recorded by Harry Nilsson in 1971.
AUNTIE GRIZELDA. From a song recorded by The Monkees. (1967).
CISCO KID. A song by the group "War" (1973).

DOG-A-MUFFIN. See "Shaggy."

FIGARO. A character in the opera "The Marriage of Figaro," by Mozart.

FOXY LADY. A song on Jimi Hendrix's 1967 debut album "Are You Experienced?"

HOUND DOG. Number one hit for Elvis Presley in 1956.

LAYLA. Song by Eric Clapton and his group Derek and the Dominos.

LEROY BROWN. "Bad, Bad, Leroy Brown" (1973). This was the number one hit for Jim Croce.

LOLA. Recorded by The Kinks in 1970; "Lola" was a cross dresser.

MIGHTY QUINN. "Quinn the Eskimo." A 1968 hit for Manfred Mann.

MR. BOJANGLES. Both The Nitty Gritty Dirt Band and Sammy Davis Jr. recorded this ditty by Jerry Jeff Walker.

PATCHES. A smash hit single in 1962 by Dickey Lee.

PRUDENCE. From the 1968 song "Dear Prudence" by John Lennon and Paul McCartney.

RHIANNON. Stevie Nicks wrote and sang this Fleetwood Mac song (1975).

ROCKET MAN. Words and music are by Elton John and Bernie Taupin (1972).

SANDY. Annie's faithful canine friend in the musical "Annie." Originally an Airedale.

SHILO. A Neil Diamond song. (1970).

MISCELLANEOUS

BACKBEAT. The stressed second and fourth beat in 4/4 time. Used in Rhythm and Blues and Rock and Roll.

BLUEGRASS. An acoustic country music genre that uses five instruments: mandolin, guitar, banjo, string bass, and fiddle.

CD. A compact disk, which is a disk of digitally encoded sound recordings.

CALYPSO. This music originating in the West Indies, is written in 2/4 time. Lyrics are sung with long vowel sounds.

CHOPSTICKS. (1877). A short composition for the piano, played with one finger of each hand.

HARMONY. The relationship of notes in the chordal structure of a musical composition.

HIP HOP. Urban street culture which includes rap music, break dancing, body popping and scratch mixing by DJs.

JAZZ. Form of music derived from African-American spirituals and blues that incorporate complex rhythms of instrumentation and improvisation.

JINGLES. Short repetitious songs used as a marketing tool on T.V. and radio commercials.

KAZOO. A small tin musical toy, in which a sound is emitted by the vibration of a breath and voice.

LULLABY. A soothing, lulling bedtime composition.

MAESTRO. A leader of musical performers; conductor of an orchestra.

OBOE. A woodwind instrument with a double reed mouthpiece and a range of 3 octaves.

PICCOLO. Flute-like instrument with a pitch that is one octave above a flute.

RAPPER. A musician who engages in rap music. "Rap" is fast-talking rhymes, spoken over a rhythm track and part of the "hip hop" culture. It started to emerge as mainstream in 1979 with Sugarhill Gang's "Rapper's Delight."

REGGAE. This is a sound, originating in Jamaica, in the 60's. Desmond Dekker's "Israelites" (1969) is an early example of Reggae. Most notable Reggae star is Bob Marley.

SLAM. Slam dancing is slamming oneself against other dancers. It was associated with the "Punk Rock" movement.

TEMPO. The rate of speed of a musical composition.

ZYDECO. Originating in Louisiana, this music is a combination of Blues and Cajun music. Instruments are usually an accordion, fiddle and guitar.

CHAPTER 8

MOVIES

MOVIE PETS

AGENT ELEVEN. Played by Bob, Agent Eleven is an FBI, drug sniffing dog who escapes protective custody in the film "See Spot Run" (2001).

ASTA. Asta is the pet terrier in the "Thin Man" detective movies starring Myrna Loy and William Powell.

BEETHOVEN. (1992). An adopted puppy that grows to be a lumbering St. Bernard in the family film "Beethoven." Stars Charles Grodin.

BENJI. A stray dog (played by the dog "Higgins") saves 2 children from being kidnapped in the family film Benji (1974).

BUDDY. The basketball-loving canine star of the movie "Air Bud" (1997). Limping toward the end of filming, he was taken to the vet and diagnosed with cancer in his rear leg. It was amputated, but he is fine, healthy and still able to shoot!

BUTKUS. Sylvester Stallone's bulldog in the 1976 movie "Rocky."

CUJO. A rabid St. Bernard traps a woman and her son at a deserted farm in this 1983 thriller. Based on the Stephen King novel.

DREYFUSS. "Bear" is the real name of the lovable St. Bernard on the T.V. series "Empty Nest" (1988-1995).

FRANKENWEENIE. (1984). Directed by Tim Burton. Sparky, the dog is brought back to life, much to the consternation of his parents.

GRUNT. Jennifer Beals' loyal pitbull terrier in the 1983 movie "Flashdance."

HOOCH. A junkyard dog who witnesses a murder in the movie "Turner and Hooch" (1989).

OLD YELLER. (1957). In this Disney tearjerker, Old Yeller contracts rabies and has to be shot by his owner.

PETEY. The dog with the circled eye, always wanted by the dog catcher on the "Our Gang" comedies.

SOUNDER. (1972). A dog owned by a sharecropper family in post depression, rural Louisiana.

MOVIE CHARACTERS

ALAMEDA SLIM. The Rotund redheaded outlaw of the animated film, "Home on the Range" (2004). Voice of Randy Quaid.

ALFALFA. Carl Switzer (1927-1959). In the "Our Gang" comedies, Alfalfa was identified with a squeaky, off-key, singing voice and a cowlick that stood straight up.

ALFIE. (1966). Michael Caine is Alfie, a pleasure seeking Casanova.

ARNOLD. Arnold Schwarzenegger (1947). Born in Austria, Arnold is a former Mr. Universe. He has appeared in the Blockbuster "Terminator" Trilogy (1984; 1999; 2003). "Total Recall" (1990) of the California governor led to Arnold being elected (2003) .

BABY DOLL. (1956). Carol Baker plays the seduced wife of Southerner. Also stars Eli Wallach and Rip Torn.

BAGGER VANCE. (2000). In the film "The Legend of Bagger Vance," Will Smith stars as the angelic golf instructor/philosopher, who guides golfer Matt Damon to victory.

BALLOU. Cat Ballou. (1965). Jane Fonda is outlaw Catherine Ballou in this western lampoon.

BOGART, HUMPHREY. (1899-1957). Played gangster roles for several years then won an academy award for "The African Queen" (1951).

BOGIE. Nickname for Humphrey Bogart.

BOWFINGER. (1999). Steve Martin, as Robert K. Bowfinger, wrote and stars in this film, as a producer who will do anything to get his movie made, including hiring a nerdy Eddie Murphy.

BRANDO. Marlon Brando (1924-). His most memorable roles were his Oscar winning roles in "On the Waterfront" (1954) and "The Godfather" (1972).

BUCKWHEAT. William Henry Thomas, Jr. (1931-1980). The Buckwheat character who wore a pigtail and was named after a breakfast food, appeared in the "Our Gang" comedies.

BUGSY. (1991). Warren Beatty and Annette Bening. Beatty is Benjamin "Bugsy" Siegel, a gangster who reportedly helped build Las Vegas.

BULL DURHAM. (1988). Kevin Costner, Susan Sarandon, Tim Robbins. Minor league baseball team Durham Bulls and groupie (Sarandon).

CHAN, CHARLIE. A detective created by author Earl Derr Biggers but based on a real life Honolulu detective named Chang Apana. Appearing in films beginning in 1926, this likeable detective solved crimes by with the help of his "#1" and "#2" sons.

CHAPLIN, CHARLIE. (1889-1977). Actor who created the beloved mustached tramp with the baggy pants, who tried to keep his dignity in a world of social injustice.

CHER. Cherilyn Sarkisian (1946-). Singer/actress who in 1988, won the Academy Award for Best Actress in "Moonstruck."

CHEWBACCA. Star Wars (1977). Lucasfilms. Chewbacca is a hundred-year-old wookie, an ape-like creature, and first noted on the spaceship Millennium Falcon in "Star Wars."

CHUCKY. A horrific doll in the three "Child's Play" movies.

COOLEY. Cooley High (1975). Comedy-drama about a high school in the 60's with a Motown soundtrack.

COOPER. Frank James Cooper (1901-1961). He won Oscars for "Sergeant York" (1942) and for "High Noon" (1952).

CORNELIUS. Roddy McDowell (1928-1998) played the sympathetic chimpanzee, Cornelius in the movie where apes are the dominant species in "Planet of the Apes" (1968).

CYBORG. (1989) Jean-Claude Van Damme plays a robot with human skin in this post-apocalyptic story.

DAMIEN. The young boy believed to be the devil in the movie "The Omen" (1976).

DARTH VADER. "Star Wars" (1977). Darth Vader directs the evil Imperial Galactic Empire. Voice of James Earl Jones.

DEMI. Demi Moore (1962-). Films include "Ghost" (1990) and "A Few Good Men" (1992).

DENZEL. Denzel Washington (1954-). Oscar winner's films include "A Soldier's Story" (1988) and "Malcolm X" (1993) and Training Day (2001).

DISNEY. Walt Disney (1901-1966). Cartoonist became successful with his film characters Mickey Mouse and Donald Duck.

DR. DOLITTLE. (1967). Rex Harrison as Dr. Dolittle, a veterinarian who enjoys tete-a-tetes with the animals.

DRACULA. (1931). Bela Lugosi plays Transylvanian vampire, Count Dracula who relocates to London and carries on in a horrific manner. Adapted from Bram Stoker's novel.

DUDLEY. Dudley Moore (1935-2002). Dudley Moore studied music at Oxford and became an accomplished classical musician. The diminutive actor's most notable movies are "10" and "Arthur."

DUMBO. (1941). In this animated Disney film, a lonely baby circus elephant learns that his assets are his ears as he learns to fly.

EWOK. "Return of the Jedi" (1983). A small bear-like creature that lives in the community of Ewoks.

FATSO. (1980). Dom LeLuise stars as "Fatso," the big kid who loved to eat, until he meets his true love.

FERRIS BUELLER. "Ferris Bueller's Day Off" (1986). Teenager (Matthew Broderick) plays truant for a day.

FLETCH. (1985). Chevy Chase plays I.M. Fletcher, a news reporter in the comedy movies "Fletch" and "Fletch Returns" (1990).

FLIM FLAM MAN. (1967). Comedy starring George C. Scott as a Southern con artist teaching his trade to an honest younger partner.

FLUBBER. (1997). An absent-minded professor discovers "flubber," a rubber-like super-bouncy substance. Stars Robin Williams.

FREEBIE. "Freebie and the Bean" (1974). Police and mobsters in this comedy starring Alan Arkin and James Caan.

FREEJACK. (1992). Racecar driver Estevez dies in 1991 and in the year 2009 his body takes up the soul of a callous businessman. Stars Emilio Estevez, Mick Jagger, Anthony Hopkins.

GARBO, GRETA. Greta Gustafsson (1905-1990). Known for her sensuality on screen and for her performance of tragic heroines "Anna Karenina" (1935) and "Camille" (1936).

GARP. "The World According to Garp" (1982). Robin Williams plays T.S. Garp with Glenn Close as his world famous feminist mother, Jenny. Based on the novel and screenplay by John Irving.

GODZILLA. (1956, 1998). A prehistoric beast who marches through Tokyo after being awakened by atomic testing.

GOLDFINGER. (1964). Sean Connery and Honor Blackman. Gold smuggler Auric Goldfinger (Gert Fröbe) runs up against James Bond, Agent 007 at Fort Knox.

GOOD BURGER. Starring T.V. sitcom friends, Kenan Thompson and Kel Mitchell. Ed's (Mitchell) special sauce makes Good Burger a winner over Mondo Burger, in this 1997 comedy film.

GREMLIN. From the Steven Spielberg movie "Gremlins" (1984). A Gremlin is a ferocious little creature who multiplies when he gets wet, and terrorizes a town.

GREYSTOKE. "Greystoke: The Legend of Tarzan, Lord of the Apes" (1984). Stars Christopher Lambert.

GROUCHO. Julius Henry "Groucho" Marx (1890-1977). Member of Marx Brothers Comedy Team. Groucho who was known for his quick wit, appeared in the films "Animal Crackers" (1930) and "Duck Soup" (1933).

HALLE. Halle Maria Berry (1968-). Golden Globe winner for "Introducing Dorothy Dandridge" (1999), and the esteemed honor of being the first African-American female to win the Best Actress Academy Award for "Monster's Ball" (2001).

HARRY POTTER. See "Literature."

HARVEY. (1950). Harvey is a 6-foot, 3-inch invisible rabbit and friend of Elwood P. Dowd (James Stewart).

HELLBOY. (2004). A demon (Ron Perlman) raised from infancy after being conjured by and rescued from the Nazis, grows up to become a defender against the forces of darkness.

HERBIE. Herbie is "The Love Bug" (1969). A Volkswagen beetle with a mind of its own.

HITCHCOCK. Alfred Hitchcock (1899-1980). Directed the suspense thrillers "Psycho" (1960) and "The Birds" (1963).

HOPALONG CASSIDY. Cowboy character created by Clarence E. Mulford. William Boyd starred as the good cowboy who wore black.

HUD. (1963). Paul Newman and Patricia Neal. Hud Bannon incites feud over fate of family ranch.

INDIANA JONES. "Raiders of the Lost Ark" (1981). Steven Spielberg adventure, starring Harrison Ford as an archaeologist overcoming constant danger in his pursuits.

JACK FROST. (1998). Michael Keaton plays a father who dies in a car accident. A year later he is resurrected as a snowman, with a chance to redeem his failure as a father.

JAKE AND ELWOOD BLUES. "The Blues Brothers" (1980). Jake (John Belushi) and Elwood (Dan Aykroyd) Blues put their old band together in hopes of saving the orphanage where they grew up.

JAMES BOND. "Bond, James Bond" is Agent 007 of British Secret Service. Bond takes on the bad guys, worldwide, in daring escapades and is always with beautiful women, unique, futuristic vehicles, and mechanical devices. From the Ian Fleming books.

JAWS. (1975). The menacing mechanical shark in the box office hit "Jaws." Roy Scheider and Richard Dreyfuss star.

JEDI. "Star Wars" (1977). Jedi Knights are galactic guardians of justice.

KING KONG. (1933). Fay Wray and Robert Armstrong. Giant ape, King Kong, terrorizes New York City, falls in love and dies atop the Empire State Building.

KINGPIN. (1996). Woody Harrelson and Randy Quaid star in this bowling "buddy movie" and literally save the family farm.

KOTCH. (1971). Walter Matthau, stars as a cantankerous grandfather at odds with his family.

LAINIE. Lainie Kazan (1942-). Singer/actress whose films include "The Crew" (2000) and "My Big Fat Greek Wedding" (2002).

LANA. Lana Turner. (1921-1995). Known as "The Sweater Girl" and World War II pinup girl. She was discovered at Schwab's Drugstore on Sunset Blvd.

LEATHERFACE. The cannibalistic maniac in "The Texas Chainsaw Massacre" (1974) was played by Gunnar Hansen II (1956-).

LITTLE MAN TATE. (1991). Directed by Jodie Foster about a child genius and his working single mother. Mother relents to placing her genius son in school for exceptional children.

LITTLE BIG MAN. (1970). Dustin Hoffman, Faye Dunaway, Martin Balsam. From Thomas Berger novel. About a pioneer and survivor of Custer's last stand.

LIZA. Liza Minnelli (1946-). She is the daughter of Judy Garland. Her father is film director Vincent Minnelli. She has won a Tony, an Oscar, and an Emmy Award.

LOST BOYS. (1987). Stars Jason Patric, Corey Haim and Dianne Wiest. "The Lost Boys" are teenage vampires in Santa Cruz, lead by Kiefer Sutherland.

MANFRED. From the movie "Ice Age" (2002). A sabertooth tiger, a sloth, and a wooly mammoth find a lost human infant, and they try to return him to his tribe. Stars Ray Romano, John Leguizamo & Denis Leary.

MCMURPHY, R.P. From "One Flew Over the Cuckoo's Nest" (1975). Jack Nicholson stars as R.P. McMurphy, a patient in an asylum who incites his fellow patients to rebel against the wretchedness of Nurse Ratched.

MINI ME. In "Austin Powers: The Spy Who Shagged Me" (1999), and "Goldmember" (2002). The diminutive Verne Troyer plays Mike Meyers' miniature version.

MISS MONEYPENNY. The faithful secretary to James Bond, 007 is the only character, besides Bond himself, to appear in every Bond film.

MISTER MAN. "Misery" (1990). James Caan, Kathy Bates. A romance novelist is the victim of an auto accident and then is cared for by psychotic fan.

MONKEYBONE. (2001). Cartoonist Stu Miley (Brendan Fraser) wakes up after a coma, possessed by the cartoon monkey he created.

MONROE, MARILYN. Norma Jean Baker (1926-1962). Blonde bombshell sex symbol whose movies include "Some Like it Hot" (1959) and "The Misfits" (1961).

MOOKIE. Spike Lee's character in the film "Do the Right Thing" (1989) where a white pizza parlor owner in black neighborhood touches off a riot.

MR. BIGGLESWORTH. The Sphynx feline star of the Austin Powers films "International Man of Mystery" (1997) and "The Spy Who Shagged Me" (1999). See "Mini Me."

MR. FREEZE. Arnold Schwarzenegger's character, Mr. Freeze/Dr. Victor Fries who wants to encase the world in ice, in "Batman & Robin" (1997).

NEO. Keanu Reeves' character with super-heroic abilities continues to battle the machines that have enslaved the human race in the "Matrix" Trilogy (1999; 2003; 2003).

NIGEL. Nigel Bruce who was famous for his role of Dr. Watson opposite Basil Rathbone, who played Sherlock in the Sherlock Holmes films in the 1940's.

OBI-WAN. (Kenobi). From "Star Wars" (1977). Alec Guinness plays Obi-Wan, who helps Luke Skywalker rescue Princess Leah.

OCTOPUSSY. (1983). James Bond film starring Roger Moore and Maud Adams. Octopussy is Major Dexter Smyth's pet of the deep blue sea and eventually the cause of his demise.

OSCAR. Annual award in the form of a gold statuette, presented by the Academy of Motion Picture Arts and Sciences for achievement in motion picture production.

OZ. "The Wizard of Oz" (1939). The Wizard of Oz is Professor Marvel in the Land of Oz in this Oscar-winning fantasy film.

POLYNESIA. The parrot that taught Dr. Dolittle to talk to the animals in the film, "Dr. Dolittle" (1967).

PUSSY GALORE. Honor Blackman plays Goldfinger's personal pilot, Pussy Galore in the James Bond film "Goldfinger."

QUIGLEY. "Quigley Down Under" (1990). Tom Selleck stars as an American cowboy who goes to Australia to work for a rancher.

RAMBO. John Rambo is a returned Vietnam vet, a fighting machine, the central character of Sylvester Stallone's action adventure "First Blood" (1982).

RATSO RIZZO. "Midnight Cowboy" (1969). This Best Picture stars Dustin Hoffman and Jon Voight as a naive male prostitute and his sickly friend who struggle to survive in the streets of New York City.

SKEET. Brian Ray "Skeet" Ulrich. (1969-). One of a group of teens (Billy Loomis) being stalked by a psychopathic serial killer in the movie "Scream" (1996).

SKYWALKER, LUKE. "Star Wars" (1977). Skywalker (Mark Hamill) rebels against the Imperial Galactic Empire.

SLAPPY. In the 1998 film "Slappy and the Stinkers," five unruly kids, dubbed "The Stinkers" by their principal, try to rescue the sea lion Slappy from an aquarium.

SMOOCHY. "Death to Smoochy" (2002). When he is fired for taking payola, the host for a children's television show plots revenge against his replacement, a rhino named Smoochy, played by Edward Norton. Also starring Robin Williams and Danny DeVito.

SPANKY. George Robert Phillips "Spanky" McFarland). (1928-1993). Appeared in "Our Gang" comedies as the chubby spokesperson.

STUART LITTLE. (1999, 2002). Stuart Little is the sweet mouse adopted by the Little family, whose presence raises the ire of the family cat. Michael J. Fox is the voice of Stuart.

SULLEY. From the movie "Monsters, Inc." (2002). John Goodman's monster character who generates city power from the bedtime screams of frightened children. Also stars Billy Crystal.

SWAYZE. Patrick Swayze (1954-). Films include "Dirty Dancing" (1987) and "Ghost" (1991).

TIBBS. Academy award winning movie "In the Heat of the Night" (1967) starring Sidney Poitier as Virgil Tibbs, a Philadelphia detective who goes to Mississippi to solve a murder with a redneck cop played by Rod Steiger.

TIN MAN. "The Wizard of Oz" (1939). Tin Man played by Jack Haley joins up with Dorothy on the way to the Emerald City.

TITUS. (1999). Loosely based on "The Tragedy of Titus Andronicus" by William Shakespeare. Anthony Hopkins stars in the role of the Roman Emperor, Titus.

TOOTSIE. (1982). Dustin Hoffman and Jessica Lange. Unemployed actor dresses as woman to land a job.

WEEBO. The robot companion of Robin Williams' character, Professor Brainard in the film "Flubber" (1997). See "Flubber."

WHOOPI. Whoopi Goldberg (1950-). Actress/Comedienne whose roles include "Sister Act" (1 and 2) and "Ghost" for which she won the Best Supporting Oscar for 1991.

WILLOW. (1988). This fantasy adventure, Willow delivers a baby to safety where it will overthrow the evil powers of Queen Bavmorda. Stars Val Kilmer.

WILLY WONKA. "Willy Wonka and the Chocolate Factory" (1971). Gene Wilder plays Willy Wonka who owns the candy factory.

YENTL. (1983). Barbra Streisand directs and stars in this story about a woman who disguises herself as a male student to study at a Yeshiva at the turn of the century.

YODA. "Return of the Jedi" (1983). Yoda was the Jedi Master.

ZOLTAR. (1998). The story of a 12-year-old boy, trying to escape the reality of his difficult family life, by believing he is an alien.

ZSA ZSA. Zsa Zsa Gabor, born Sari Gabor (1916-). After many roles and notable marriages, she has come to be currently married to Prince Frederick von Anhalt, the Duke of Saxony.

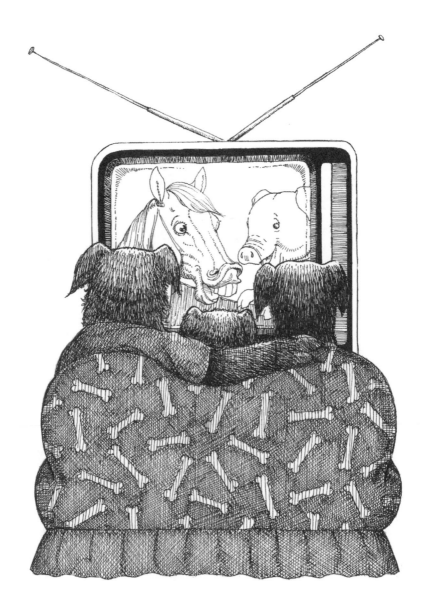

CHAPTER 9

TELEVISION

T. V. PETS

APOLLO. One of two menacing Dobermans owned by Robin Masters, a wealthy estate owner in "Magnum, P.I".

ARNOLD. The lovable pig in the comedy series "Green Acres" (1965-1971).

BUCK. The Bundy family pet played by a dog named "Michael" on the series "Married with Children" (1987-1997).

CLEO. The talking basset hound, on the sitcom "The People's Choice" (1955-1958) starring Jackie Cooper. Voice of Mary Jane Croft.

DIEFENBAKER. Faithful companion to Paul Gross' character Benton Fraser on the T.V. show "Due South" (1994-1998). "Draco" is the real name of Diefenbaker.

DREYFUSS. Dreyfuss is Dr. Harry Weston's St. Bernard on the sitcom "Empty Nest" (1988-1995). Dreyfuss is played by "Bear."

HAPPY. As himself, plays the white terrier/mix Camden family dog on the WB's "7th Heaven."

LADADOG. Ladadog was the sheepdog in the T.V. series "Please Don't Eat the Daisies" (1965-1967). "Lord Nelson" played Ladadog.

LASSIE. The well-known collie, was at least six different dogs over the years (1954-1974).

MAX. Max the bulldog, in the T.V. series "Jake and the Fatman" (1987-1992) is played by "Buford."

MCDUFF. McDuff is a ghostly English sheepdog who can only be seen and heard by his veterinarian in "McDuff, the Talking Dog" (1976). Voice of Jack Lester.

MORRIS, THE CAT. Whose real name is "Lucky." Is there a more finicky cat?

MRS. WHISKERSON. On an episode of "Friends" (1994-) Rachel (Jennifer Aniston) buys herself a hairless sphinx cat she names Mrs. Whiskerson, but the cat is mean so Rachel has to sell her.

QUARK. Dog on the T.V. show "Honey, I Shrunk the Kids" (1997-).

RIN TIN TIN. Star of the western series "Rin Tin Tin" (1954-1959). This German shepherd and his master, Rusty (Lee Aaker) joined the 101st Cavalry after an Indian raid on wagon trains.

SHAMSKY. This bulldog belongs to Ray "Barone" Romano's brother, Robert in "Everybody Loves Raymond" (1996-).

SIGMUND. Lucy Coe's (Lynn Herring) pet duck on the daytime drama "Port Charles."

SOCK PUPPET. The spokes-dog for the former website "pets.com" who was often seen driving around town, saying, "I'm a professional happy puppet thing!" and "I'm here to play with the tabby cat!"

TRIGGER. Trigger was the horse ridden by Roy Rogers on the contemporary western "The Roy Rogers Show."

WISHBONE. This intelligent Jack Russell Terrier is named for the PBS series designed to introduce children to classic literature and the love of reading books.

ZEUS. See "Apollo."

T. V. CHARACTERS

99. Agent 99, an intelligence agent played by Barbara Feldon, opposite Don Adams, who played Maxwell Smart in the comedy series "Get Smart" (1965-1969).

ANDROMEDA. (2000-). Gene Rodenberry inspired sci-fi T.V. series, starring Kevin Sorbo as Captain Dylan Hunt.

ARTEMUS. Artemus Gordon (Ross Martin) is associate to Secret Service agent James West (Robert Conrad) in the T.V. western "The Wild, Wild West" (1965-1969).

B.J. B.J. (Billie Joe) McKay is a trucker, played by Greg Evigan, in the adventure series "B.J. and the Bear".

BABA WAWA. A character played by Gilda Radner on "Saturday Night Live," spoofing broadcast journalist Barbara Walters.

BALKI. Balki Bartokomous (Bronson Pinchot), is the bewildered, foreign cousin in the sitcom "Perfect Strangers" (1986-1993).

BARNABY JONES. Buddy Ebsen plays private eye "Barnaby Jones" (1973-1980).

BEAVER. Jerry Mathers plays "The Beaver," the youngest son of the all-American family, the Cleavers in the sitcom "Leave it to Beaver" (1957-1963).

BENSON. Robert Guillaume is Benson who goes from managing a governor's household to being elected Lieutenant Governor, himself.

BILKO. Master Sergeant Ernie Bilko was masterfully played by Phil Silvers on "The Phil Silvers Show" (1955-1959).

BINGHAMTON. Joe Flynn (1925-1974) played Captain Wallace Binghamton on "McHale's Navy," a sitcom set in the Pacific during World War II.

BIXBY. Bill Bixby (1934-1993). Actor/director, whose many T.V. series include "The Courtship of Eddie's Father," "My Favorite Martian," "The Magician" and "The Incredible Hulk".

BLOSSOM. (1990-1995). Blossom Russo, played by Mayim Bialik (1975-) is a teenager who lives with her brothers and divorced father in this sitcom.

BOOM BOOM. Freddie "Boom Boom" Washington (Lawrence Hilton-Jacobs) is a "Sweathog" at James Buchanan High in the sitcom "Welcome Back, Kotter" (1975-1979).

BOSLEY. David Doyle plays the liaison in "Charlie's Angels" (1976-1981).

BOZO. "Bozo the Clown" was the animated children's clown.

BRADY. The sitcom "The Brady Bunch" starred Florence Henderson, a widow with 3 daughters who marries Robert Reed, a widower with 3 sons (1969-1974).

BUFFY. "Buffy the Vampire Slayer" (1997-) stars Sarah Michelle Gellar as the only woman in the world capable of killing vampires.

BULL. Richard Moll played the goofy bailiff Bull on "Night Court" (1984-1992).

BUNDY. The last name of the family in the slightly offensive sitcom "Married with Children" (1987-1997).

BURT. Burt Campbell (Richard Mulligan), a character among the dysfunctional families of the comedy series "Soap" (1977-1981).

CANNON. (1971-1976). William Conrad stars as Frank Cannon, a private eye, in the crime show drama.

CHICO. "Chico and the Man," a sitcom set in East Los Angeles, starred Freddie Prinze and Jack Albertson.

COLONEL KLINK. German actor, Werner Klemperer (1920-2000) plays Colonel Wilhelm Klink, commandant of Stalag 13 in the hit T.V. series "Hogan's Heroes" (1965-1971).

COLUMBO. Peter Falk plays Columbo, a police lieutenant investigating crimes in his seemingly awkward manner, on the series "Columbo" (1971-1978, 1989-1997).

CONEHEAD. Created on "Saturday Night Live," "The Coneheads" (Beldar and Prymaat) were a family from the planet Remulak who had cone-shaped heads. Played by Dan Aykroyd and Jane Curtin.

CORKY. Corky Sherwood, an air-head journalist from the "Murphy Brown" (1988-1998) sitcom played by Faith Ford.

CROCKETT. Sonny Crockett (Don Johnson) was a vice cop on "Miami Vice" (1984-1989).

CUBBY. Carl "Cubby" O'Brien, a mouseketeer from the original series the "Mickey Mouse Club" (1955-1959).

CYBORG. (1973). Title of the pilot movie for the T.V. show that came to be called "The Six Million Dollar Man." (1974-1978). Lee Majors stars as Colonel Steve Austin who is reconstructed with bionic limbs after a near fatal plane crash.

D.J. "Dinna Jean" (Candace Cameron) is the eldest sister on the sitcom "Full House" (1987-1995).

DABNEY. Dabney Coleman starred as "Buffalo Bill" (1983) and "Madman of the People" (1994-1995).

DATA. Brent Spiner (1949-) plays Lt. Commander Data, the humanoid that wants to learn to be more human. Star Trek: The Next Generation (1987-1994).

DAUBER. Dauber Dybinski (Bill Fagerbakke) is student assistant to football coach Hayden Fox (Craig T. Nelson) on the sitcom "Coach" (1989-1997).

DIETER. Mike Meyers plays Dieter, the avant-garde German host of "Sprockets" segment on "Saturday Night Live."

DIXIE. Dixie Carter (1939-) starred in the sitcom "Designing Women" as Julia Sugarbaker, one of a team of interior designers (1986-1993) and on "Family Law" (1999-).

DOBIE GILLIS. Dwayne Hickman starred as Dobie (1959-1963).

DOOGIE HOWSER. Neil Patrick Harris played Douglas "Doogie" Howser, a 16-year-old physician, on the comedy series "Doogie Howser, M.D." (1989-1993).

DR. KILDARE. (1961-1966). Richard Chamberlain starred as Dr. James Kildare.

EL-TRAIN. Steven Daniel plays this slow but smooth character, Lionel on "City Guys" (1997-2002).

ELDIN. Robert Pastorelli is Eldin, the painter, artist, nanny and philosopher-in-residence in the sitcom "Murphy Brown" (1988-1998).

ELVIRA. Cassandra "Mistress of the Dark" Peterson. (1951-). Beautiful black-dressed hostess of "Movie Macabre," she is horror movies' Queen of the Night.

ETHEL. Vivian Vance is the ever-present neighbor and partner in crime on the classic "I Love Lucy." See "Lucy."

FESTER. Uncle Fester, played by Jackie Coogan is a member of the ghastly, fit for Halloween "Addams Family" (1964-1966).

FESTUS. Festus Haggen (Ken Curtis) became the deputy of Dodge City in the longest running T.V. western "Gunsmoke" (1955-1975).

FLIP. Flip Wilson, comedian, known among other things for the character Geraldine, popularized on his program "The Flip Wilson Show" (1970-1974).

FLIPPER. (1964-1967). A lovable dolphin on the series "Flipper".

FONZIE. Arthur "Fonzie" Fonzarelli, the charming and all around cool dude in the sitcom "Happy Days". Played by Henry Winkler (1974-1984).

FRED. The cantankerous neighbor, Fred Mertz (William Frawley) in the "I Love Lucy" series (1951-1957). See "Lucy."

GERALDO. Geraldo Rivera (1943-). Journalist, attorney and indomitable talk show host.

GIDGET. Sally Field was "Gidget" (girl midget) in this "surf's up" series (1965-1966).

GILDA. Gilda Radner (1946-1989). Wild and funny comedienne, best known for her characters from the T.V. show "Saturday Night Live" Roseanne Rosannadanna, Emily Litella, and of course, Baba Wawa.

GILLIGAN. The likeable, dizzy first mate of the Minnow is stranded on "Gilligan's Island" with The Professor, The Skipper, The Millionaire and others. Bob Denver is Gilligan (1964-1967).

GOMER PYLE. Gomer Pyle, U.S.M.C. (1964-1970). Jim Nabors (1930-) as Gomer Pyle, the gas station attendant in Mayberry on "The Andy Griffith Show" (1963-1964) and then he later joined the Marine Corp.

GOMEZ. Gomez Addams is the patriarch of the weird "Addams Family." John Astin is Gomez (1964-1966).

GONZO. Gregory Harrison plays Dr. G. Alonzo Gates, an arrogant young doctor on the hospital drama "Trapper John, M.D." (1979-1986).

GOOBER. George Lindsey plays Goober Pyle, Gomer's cousin in "The Andy Griffith Show."

GOPHER. Burl "Gopher" Smith "Your Yeoman Purser" on the "Love Boat" (1977-1986). Played by Fred Grandy.

GRADY. Grady is the crusty pal of Fred Sanford in the sitcom "Sanford and Son" (1972-1977).

HAWK. Avery Brooks. Hawk ("Spen-sah") co-stars with Robert Urich in the detective series "Spenser for Hire" (1985-1988).

HAWKEYE. Captain Benjamin Franklin (Hawkeye) Pierce is an army surgeon doing a tour of duty in a "M.A.S.H". Unit during the Korean War. Stars Alan Alda (1972-1983).

HAZEL. (1961-1966). Shirley Booth played the maid who couldn't mind her own business.

HIGGINS. Jonathan Quayle Higgins III, played by Jonathan Hillerman, is Robin Masters' persnickety attendant in "Magnum P. I."

HOGAN. The sitcom "Hogan's Heroes" has Colonel Robert Hogan (Bob Crane) in a German POW camp during World War II (1965-1971).

HOMEY THE CLOWN. This cantankerous clown was a regular feature of the comedy series "In Living Color" played by Damon Wayans (1990-1994).

HORSHACK. Arnold Horshack (Ron Palillo) is an underachieving student, a "Sweathog" in the sitcom "Welcome Back Kotter" (1975-1979).

HOSS. Hoss rides with the Cartwright men across the "Bonanza" landscape. Dan Blocker played Hoss (1959-1972).

HOULIHAN. "Hot Lips" Houlihan or Major Margaret Houlihan (Loretta Swit), head nurse and girlfriend of whiny, married Major Frank Burns in "M.A.S.H."

HOWDY DOODY. The freckle-faced "Howdy Doody" lived in Doodyville, boys and girls. (1947-1970).

HUGGIE BEAR. Antonio Fargas played the street-smart and funny snitch Huggie Bear in the T.V. series "Starsky and Hutch" (1975-1979).

HUNTER. (1984-1991). Police show set at LAPD starring Fred Dryer as Sergeant Rick Hunter and Stepfanie Kramer as Sergeant Dee Dee McCall.

HUTCH. David Soul is Ken Hutchinson, an undercover cop. See "Starsky."

IGNATOWSKI. Jim Ignatowski, the disheveled, stupefied yet literate cabdriver and sometime "Reverend," was played by Christopher Lloyd on the sitcom "Taxi" (1979-1983).

J.J. Jimmie Walker (1947-) is J.J., the jive talking son in the sitcom "Good Times" (1974-1975).

J.R. The conniving, amoral character John Ross Ewing (Larry Hagman) is the eldest son of the wealthy Ewing family on the drama series "Dallas" (1978-1991).

JETHRO. Jethro Bodine (Max Baer, Jr.) is the nephew of Jed Clampett (Buddy Ebsen) in the "Beverly Hillbillies" (1962-1971).

JIMINY GLICK. Primetime Glick (2001). As comedian Martin Short's puffed out alter ego, Jiminy's gross incompetence, and clueless confidence shine in conversations with various celebrities.

KABLAM! (1996-1998). The Nickelodeon comic book T.V. show with cartoon characters Henry and June.

KELSO. Ashton Kutcher plays Michael Kelso in the show that relives the angst of 1970's teenager in "That 70's Show" (1998-).

KENAN & KEL. Kenan Thompson and Kel Mitchell are the duo of the Nickelodeon programs "All That," "Kenan and Kel" and the film "Good Burger."

KLINGER. Jamie Farr was Corporal Max Klinger, who persistently dressed in drag in hopes of getting booted out of the military in the comedy series "M.A.S.H."

KLINGON. The Klingon Empire harbors a race that explores and conquers others with no qualms in science fiction series "Star Trek."

KNUCKLEHEAD. Knucklehead Smiff, a dummy created by ventriloquist Paul Winchell, who appeared along with dummy Jerry Mahoney on various T.V. variety shows in the 1950's and 1960's.

KUBIAC. Larry Kubiac (Abraham Benrubi) is the high school jock in the sitcom "Parker Lewis Can't Lose" (1990-1993).

LARUE. Lynette Winter played Larue, Gidget's girlfriend in "Gidget."

LOVEY. Mrs. Howell was one of the shipwrecked characters on "Gilligan's Island" (1964-1967). She is married to millionaire, Thurston Howell III. Natalie Schafer played Lovey.

LUCY. The wacky Lucy Ricardo (Lucille Ball) of "I Love Lucy" fame (1951-1957).

LUMPY. Clarence "Lumpy" Rutherford (Frank Bank) is a friend of "The Beav" on "Leave it to Beaver" (1957-1963).

MACGYVER. (1985-1992). Richard Dean Anderson (1950-) played an agent for a foundation that ran secret missions for the government.

MAGNUM. (1980-1988). A private investigator, Thomas Sullivan Magnum (Tom Selleck), solves crimes in Hawaii on "Magnum, P.I."

MANNIX. (1967-1975). Joe Mannix (Mike Connors) is a private eye in Los Angeles, on the series "Mannix."

MAUDE. (1972-1978). Beatrice Arthur plays a very vocal Maude Findlay of Tuckahoe in "Maude."

MAVERICK. (1957-1962). A western starring James Garner as Bret Maverick.

MAX HEADROOM. (1987). Computer generated character "Max Headroom" was the alter ego of a T.V. reporter played by Matt Frewer.

MAXWELL SMART. Don Adams played Maxwell Smart, Secret Agent 86, bungling through his assignments against evil KAOS in the series "Get Smart" (1965-1970).

MAYNARD G. KREBBS. Bongo-beating beatnik of the program "Dobie Gillis" played by Bob Denver (1959-1963).

MCCLOUD. (1970-1977). Sam McCloud (Dennis Weaver) is a deputy Marshall from New Mexico, learning to fight crime in New York.

MIKEY. Renowned commercial of "Life Cereal" in the 1960's. Mikey's brothers say, "Ask Mikey, he eats everything." Then after seeing Mikey eating his cereal, they exclaim, "Hey, he likes it!"

MILES. Grant Shoud is the neurotic news producer Miles Silverberg on "Murphy Brown" (1988-1998).

MISS BROOKS. Eve Arden played Connie Brooks, a high school teacher in the sitcom "Our Miss Brooks" (1952-1956).

MISS KITTY. Kitty Russell (Amanda Blake) ran the Long Branch Saloon in Dodge City, on the western "Gunsmoke" (1955-1975).

MISTER ED. (1961-1966). A talking horse, of course, starred in this comedy series. Allan "Rocky" Lane was the voice of Mister Ed

MOESHA. Recording artist Brandy Norwood stars as the teenager Moesha Mitchell in this comedy series (1996-2001).

MOONDOGGIE. Moondoggie is a surfer and heartthrob on the T.V. series "Gidget."

MORK. Mork is an alien who has come to earth to learn about humans. Robin Williams starred in the sitcom "Mork and Mindy" (1978-1982).

MORTICIA. The ghastly pallored mother in the eccentric "Addams Family" played by Carolyn Jones (1964-1966).

MR. BEAN. English actor Rowan Sebastian Atkinson (1955-) with the agile face and body plays the incorrigible "Mr. Bean" in the British television series and film (1997).

MR. ROGERS. Fred Rogers has for years been a guidance to children on "Mr. Rogers' Neighborhood," the longest running children's program on public television.

MR. T. Known for lots of brawn and jewelry, Lawrence "Mr. T." Tero, starred as B.A. Barracus on the series "The A Team" (1983-1987).

MRS. PIGGLE-WIGGLE (1994). From the children's books by Betty MacDonald. Jean Stapleton stars as the woman who cures children of bad behavior such as talking back and bad table manners.

MS. MUSSO. Ms. Musso is the principal on the comedy series "Parker Lewis Can't Lose" (1990-1993). Melanie Chartoff played Ms. Musso.

MUNCH. Detective John Munch is the dour, albeit politically savvy cop on both Homicide: Life on the Street (1993-1999) and Law & Order, Special Victim's Unit (2000-). Played by Richard Belzer.

MURDOCH. Rupert Murdoch, a media mogul who established a fourth television network for America in 1986, the Fox Television Network.

MURPHY BROWN. (1988-1998). The aggressively assertive female T.V. journalist on the sitcom "Murphy Brown". Candice Bergen played "Murphy."

NILES. Psychiatrist Niles Crane, brother of Dr. Frasier Crane of "Frasier" (1994-).

NORM. Perennially unemployed, Norm Peterson (George Wendt) warms a barstool at "Cheers" (1982-1993).

NORTON. Art Carney was the bungling neighbor, Ed Norton on the now nostalgic comedy series "The Honeymooners" (1952-1957).

OPIE. Opie Taylor is the son of Sheriff Andy Taylor of Mayberry in "The Andy Griffith Show." Ron Howard played Opie (1960-1968).

PARKER. "Parker Lewis Can't Lose" in his adventures as a mischievous student at Santa Domingo High School. Corin Nemec played Parker (1990-1993).

PONCH. Erik Estrada played a California motorcycle highway patrolman, Francis "Ponch" Poncharello on the action series "CHIPS" (1977-1983).

POTSIE. Warren "Potsie" Webber (Anson Williams) is one of Richie's friends on "Happy Days" (1974-1984).

PUGSLEY. The son of Gomez and Morticia of "The Addams Family" (1964-1966). Pugsley was played by Ken Weatherwax.

PUNKY. An abandoned little girl is found by a building manager who becomes her guardian on the sitcom "Punky Brewster" (1984-1988). Soleil Moon Frye played Punky.

QUARK. Ferengi businessman who lived for the acquisition of bars of platinum in the sci-fi T.V. series "Star Trek: Deep Space Nine" (1993-1999). Armin Shimerman played the hard-working Quark.

QUINCY. (1976-1983). As Medical Examiner for the LA County Coroner's Office, Dr. Quincy often did further investigations of circumstances. Jack Klugman played Quincy.

RADAR. Corporal Walter "Radar" O'Reilly is the unaffected clerk and communications person of the MASH Unit in the series "M.A.S.H." Played by Gary Burghoff.

REMINGTON STEELE. (1982-1987). Pierce Brosnan co-starred with Stephanie Zimbalist as "Remington Steele" in this detective program.

RERUN. Fred Berry (1951-) played the boisterous character in the 1970's sitcom "What's Happening?"

RICKY. Bandleader Ricky Ricardo (Desi Arnaz). "Babalou" was husband of zany Lucy in "I Love Lucy" (1951-1957).

RILEY. Riley was a riveter at an aircraft plant in the sitcom "The Life of Riley." William Bendix played Riley (1953-1958).

ROCHESTER. Rochester Van Jones plays valet to comedian Jack Benny on "The Jack Benny Show". Rochester's real name was Eddie Anderson (1950-1965).

ROCKFORD. Private eye Jim Rockford solves crimes out of his trailer in Malibu. James Garner starred in "The Rockford Files" (1974-1980).

ROPER. Stanley Roper (Norman Fell) is the clueless landlord in the sitcom "Three's Company" (1977-1979).

SABRINA. "Sabrina, the Teenage Witch" stars Melissa Joan Hart. (1996-2003).

SALEM. Nick Bakay is the voice of the mechanical black cat on the "Sabrina, the Teenage Witch" series (1996-2003).

SAMMO. Sammo Law (1952-). Sammo Hung Kam-Bo, a Chinese cop and hand combat instructor comes to Los Angeles and is partnered with American cops in the T.V. show Martial Law (1998-2000).

SCREECH. Screech is a nerd at Bayside High School on "Saved By the Bell" (1989-1993). Dustin Diamond played Screech.

SEINFELD. (1989-1998). The hit T.V. show about "nothing" and the everyday life of four New Yorkers: Jerry, George, Elaine and Kramer. Starred comedian Jerry Seinfeld.

SIMKA. Presumably from somewhere in Eastern Europe, Simka, married to Latka had a ditzy personality and a voice to match. Carol Kane played Simka on the sitcom "Taxi" (1978-1983).

SIX. Jennifer Jean "Jenna" von Oÿ (1977-) played the animated best friend of Blossom Russo on the sitcom "Blossom" (1991-1995).

SKIPPY. Skippy is the neighbor to the Keaton family in the sitcom "Family Ties" (1982-19189). Played by Marc Price.

SLATER. A.C. Slater (Mario Lopez) is buddy to Zack Morris at Bayside High School on the Saturday morning sitcom "Saved By the Bell" (1989-1993).

SPENSER. Robert Urich played Boston private eye Spenser in "Spenser: For Hire" (1985-1988).

SPOCK. Leonard Nimoy is Science Officer Spock, and Vulcan on the Starship Enterprise in the series "Star Trek" (1966-1969).

SQUIGGY. Andrew "Squiggy" Squigman played by David L. Lander, on the sitcom "Laverne and Shirley," was usually seen with Lenny, his co-worker, played by Michael McKean.

STARSKY. Paul Michael Glaser played Dave Starsky, an undercover policeman on the series "Starsky and Hutch" (1975-1979).

STYMIE. Matthew Beard (1925-1981). The derby wearing "Little Rascal" who was everybody's best friend.

SWOOSIE. Swoosie Kurtz (1944-). Swoosie was named after the B-17 bomber "The Swangoose" that was piloted by her father (a decorated WWII bomber pilot). She played eldest sister Alex in T.V. series "Sisters" (1991-1996).

T.C. Theodore Calvin (Roger Mosley) charters helicopters in "Magnum, P.I.," and is a buddy to Thomas Magnum (1980-1988).

TABITHA. Daughter of Samantha and Darrin Stephens on "Bewitched". Tabitha had the same bewitching powers as her mother (1964-1972).

TATTOO. An assistant to Mr. Roarke, Herve Villechaize played Tattoo on "Fantasy Island" (1978-1983), an island where dreams came true.

THEO. Malcolm-Jamal Warner played Theodore Huxtable, son of Dr. Huxtable on the sitcom "The Cosby Show" (1984-1992).

TOMA. (1973-1974). Newark Police Department detective "Toma" which starred Tony Musante.

TONTO. Jay Silverheels was Tonto, The Lone Ranger's scout in the popular western "The Lone Ranger" (1947-1957).

TOPO GIGO. Italian puppet, Topo Gigo is a mouse. He appeared on "The Ed Sullivan Show" for the first time, April 14, 1963.

TRAPPER JOHN. Captain John Francis Xavier McIntire, aka Trapper John (Wayne Rogers) wielded the scalpel alongside Hawkeye Pierce in "M.A.S.H." (1972-1975). Pernell Roberts went on to star in the spin-off "Trapper John, M.D" (1979-1986).

TRIBBLE. Small furry creature detested by the Klingons in the Sci-fi series "Star Trek."

TRIPPER. Jack Tripper (John Ritter) is a chef who lives with 2 female roommates in the sitcom "Three's Company" (1977-1984).

TUBBS. Detective Ricardo Tubbs in the police drama "Miami Vice" (1984-1989). Philip Michael Thomas played Tubbs. See "Crockett."

UNCLE MILTIE. (1908-2002) Milton Berle, a vaudevillian that hosted radio and T.V. shows from the 1940's to 1967.

URKEL. Steve Urkel is the nerd with the irritating voice and high-belted pants in the sitcom "Family Matters" (1989-1998). Jaleel White played Steve Urkel.

VULCAN. Vulcans are a race of people who utilize logic and become peaceful through the control of their emotions. See "Star Trek."

WALDO. Waldo Geraldo Faldo (Shawn Harrison I) of the sitcom "Family Matters" (1990-1996). Waldo was the oft-clueless friend of Eddie Winslow (Darius McCrary).

WALLY. Wally Cleaver (Tony Dow) is the older brother and confidante to "The Beaver" on the sitcom "Leave it to Beaver" (1957-1963).

WEBSTER. An African-American orphan, Webster (Emmanuel Lewis) is cared for by a Caucasian couple in the sitcom of the same name (1983-1988).

WEDNESDAY. Wednesday is the daughter in the ghastly "Addams Family" (1964-1966) sitcom. Lisa Loring played Wednesday.

WILBUR. Wilbur Post played by Alan Young, discovers Mister Ed, the talking horse in the sitcom "Mister. Ed" (1961-1966).

WILLARD. Weatherman Willard Scott (1934-) is with NBC's morning program "The Today Show," where he also celebrates the birthdays of centenarians.

WIZZO, THE WIZARD. Character on "Bozo the Clown."

WOODY. Woody is the easy-going Mid-Western bartender on "Cheers" (1985-1996), affectionately played by Woody Harrelson.

XENA. Lucy Lawless is Xena, the chakram-throwing defender of good against evil in the mytho/historical T.V. series "Xena: Warrior Princess" (1995-2001).

Atomic Hampster™

Liberating hampsters everywhere!

CHAPTER 10

CARTOONS AND COMIC STRIP CHARACTERS

ALLEY OOP. Alley Oop is a cave man who romps with the dinosaurs. This character, created by V.T. Hamlin, first appeared in 1933.

ALVIN. One of the chipmunks in "The Alvin Show" which was an adaptation of the novelty song by Ross Bagdasarian "The Chipmunk Song."

ARCHIE. Archie is forever a student at Riverdale High along with Jughead, Betty, Reggie and others from the comic strip "Archie" by Bob Montana.

ASTRO. "The Jetson's" pet dog.

AUGIE DOGGIE. From the Hanna-Barbera series "Augie Doggie and Doggie Daddy." Augie Doggie is forever flattering Doggie Daddy to make up for his mischievous ways. Daws Butler was the voice of Augie.

B.C. A stone-age comic strip started in 1958 by Johnny Hart. Characters include Grog, Tor and Clumsy Carp.

BABY BOP. A sweet natured, three year-old triceratops, Baby Bop is one of Barney's best friends in the children's series about the purple dinosaur who loves everyone.

BABY HUEY. Oversized baby duck created by Paramount Famous Studios. This lumbering duck is usually able to obstruct the preying fox.

BAMM BAMM. Son of Bedrock's Barney & Betty Rubble in the prehistoric "Flintstones" series.

BARNEY. Barney and Betty Rubble are neighbors of Fred and Wilma Flintstone in Bedrock. The stone-age cartoon series "The Flintstones" were modeled after the T.V. program "The Honeymooners." Mel Blanc was the voice of Barney.

BART. Member of the bug-eyed, gauche Simpson family created by Matt Groenig.

BATMAN. The Caped Crusader first appeared in D.C. Comics in 1939. He resides in Gotham City and fights villains.

BEETLE BAILEY. The soldier, with his hat permanently affixed over his eyes, actually started out as a college student by the name of Spider. Mort Walker transformed the character to a soldier and "Beetle Bailey" was a smash hit.

BERT. A member of the Muppet duo Bert and Ernie of "Sesame Street" fame, Bert has the vertical head, vertically striped shirt and one long eyebrow.

BLONDIE. The beautiful, svelte wife of Dagwood Bumstead in the comic strip "Blondie" and T.V. series "Blondie and Dagwood."

BLUTO. Bluto is Popeye's rival for the affections of Olive Oyl in the Popeye Cartoons. Bluto is no match for Popeye when Popeye gulps his spinach.

BONZO. A mischievous bull pup created by George Ernest Studdy, a British cartoonist after World War I.

BOO BOO. Sidekick and partner in crime to Yogi Bear at Jellystone National Park. Voice of Don Messick.

BORIS. Boris Badenov, a Russian agent of Mr. Big in "The Bullwinkle Show." Voice of Paul Frees.

BUGS. The brazen rabbit and all-around wise guy. Animators at Warner Brothers Cartoon Studio created bugs Bunny.

BULLWINKLE. Originally created for the comic strip "Bullwinkle" by Jay Ward. Bullwinkle Moose starred alongside Rocky, the flying squirrel in "Rocky and His Friends" and then the "Bullwinkle Show" (1959-1963). Voice of Bill Scott.

BUZZ LIGHTYEAR. The space-ranger toy in the film "Toy Story" (1995). Tim Allen is the voice of Buzz.

CAPTAIN KANGAROO. (1955-1984). Children's T.V. show hosted by Bob Keeshan.

CAPTAIN NEMO. Captain Nemo is the captain of the Nautilus in the undersea journey to find the lost continent of Atlantis from the Jules Verne novel "20,000 Leagues Under the Sea."

CHILLY WILLY. The lovable penguin from the Walter Lantz studio of cartoons.

CLARK KENT. The mild mannered reporter at the "Daily Planet" who transforms himself into Superman from the planet Krypton.

CLIFFORD. Clifford is PBS' favorite "Big Red Dog."

CLUMSY CARP. See BC.

CRUELLA DE VIL. The villainess in Disney's "The 101 Dalmatians" from the children's novel by Dodie Smith. Cruella planned to make fur coats from the Dalmatians.

CRUSADER RABBIT. Created by Jay Ward and Alexander Anderson, Jr. Crusader Rabbit was usually attired in armor sitting atop his horse in Galahad Glen. Voice of Lucille Bliss.

DAGWOOD. The bungling husband and father, Dagwood Bumstead was created by Chic Young for his comic strip "Blondie."

DEPUTY DAWG. A dog of a sheriff tries to maintain law and disorder in Mississippi. Voice of Dayton Allen.

DINO. The prehistoric, pink dinosaur pet of the Flintstones.

DOC. Bespectacled Doc is considered the leader of the seven dwarfs in "Snow White and the Seven Dwarfs," even with his dithering style of speaking.

DOGGIE DADDY. See Auggie Doggie.

DONATELLO. One of the four Teenage Mutant Ninja Turtles who are the pizza eating, wise cracking teenage turtles with a talent for martial arts.

DONDI. 1955-1986. Dondi by Gus Edson and drawn by Irwin Hasen.

DOONESBURY. "Doonesbury" a cartoon of political and satirical commentary, by Garry Trudeau (1970-).

DRABBLE. A daily comic strip by Kevin Fagan.

DROOPY. A dog created by Tex Avery. He first appeared as a police dog in the cartoon "Dumb-Hounded" (1943).

DUDLEY DO RIGHT. Canadian Mountie to the rescue in "The Bullwinkle Show." Voice of Bill Scott.

ELMER FUDD. Armed and forever on the hunt for Bugs Bunny, Elmer Fudd is always outsmarted by the "Cwazy Wabbit."

ELMO. Elmo is red and furry and one of the Muppets.

ERNIE. The other half of the Muppet duo Bert and Ernie of "Sesame Street" fame. Ernie has the horizontal head and stripes and no eyebrows.

FANTASIA. When released in November 1940, this full-length film successfully combined animation with classical music.

FELIX. The character Felix the Cat (1958-1960) was originally animated by Otto Messmer. In this 1958-1960 cartoon. Felix is accessorized by a bag of magic tricks. '

FIEVEL. Fievel Mousekewitz, a mouse, comes to America with his family from Russia in the Don Bluth feature cartoon "An American Tail."

FRITZ. Fritz the Cat, considered an underground comic strip, was written by Robert Crumb (1968). Fritz a womanizer, is a humanized Tom Cat who is always on the make.

GARFIELD. The comic strip cat created by Jim Davis, who is a human-like fat cat that dislikes cat food, dogs and diets.

GATOR. Hanna-Barbera production. Wally Gator is an alligator that doesn't like the zoo.

GIGANTOR. A robot, propelled through space to fight evil with the help of a 12 year-old.

GOOFY. Originally known as Dippy Dawg, Goofy is a Mickey Mouse cohort.

GROG. See "BC."

GRUMPY. Cranky Grumpy is the disagreeable dwarf in Disney's "Snow White" but eventually does prove charming.

GUMBY. An odd-shaped, walking, talking, green clay figure that first appeared on the "Howdy Doody" program. In 1957, Gumby and Pokey (his pet horse) had their own program "The Gumby Show." Voice of Art Clokey.

HAGAR. Hagar the Horrible (1973) is a boorish Viking created by Dik Browne.

HEATHCLIFF. (1973-). Created by George Gately, Heathcliff is a spoiled cat who thinks he owns the house as well as the neighborhood.

HOMER PIGEON. Walter Lantz created this character based on Red Skelton's Clem Kadiddlehopper (1942). Voice of Dal McKennon.

HOPPER. Kevin Spacey was the voice of "Hopper" in the film "A Bug's Life" (1998).

HUCKLEBERRY HOUND. A bloodhound with a southern accent starred with Pixie and Dixie and Yogi Bear in the "Huckleberry Hound Show." Voice of Daws Butler.

IGNATZ. The antagonist of Krazy Kat, this mouse is oftentimes seen heaving a brick at Krazy Kat.

JERRY. The mouse who continuously thwarts Tom in their cat and mouse game in "Tom and Jerry."

JETSON. In contrast to the stone-age "Flintstones" Hanna-Barbera created the space-age family "The Jetsons" (1962) replete with futuristic technology

JUGHEAD. Friend of Archie and a student at Riverdale High in the Archie comic strip and T.V. cartoon. Voice of Howard Morris.

KERMIT. Kermit the famous Muppet frog, was a cast member of "Sesame Street."

KRAZY KAT. (1911). Created by George Herriman, this comic strip had basically three characters: Offissa Pup, Krazy Kat and Ignatz who were usually in pursuit of each other.

LARIAT PETE. First comic strip by George Herriman.

LARIAT SAM. This was a cartoon character appearing on the children's T.V. show "Captain Kangaroo."

LEONARDO. One of the four Teenage Mutant Ninja Turtles. See "Donatello."

LIL' ABNER. The beefy hillbilly who romps with the scantily clad Daisy Mae in Dogpatch. Created by Al Capp (1934).

LINUS. The "Peanuts" character who never lets his blanket down and makes it okay to suck your thumb.

MAGILLA GORILLA. In the "Magilla Gorilla Show," Magilla lives in Mr. Peebles pet shop who goes off on adventures. Voice of Allan Melvin.

MAGPIE. Blackbirds Heckle and Jeckle.

MARMADUKE. The havoc-wreaking Great Dane created by Bradley Anderson.

MARVIN. Marvin Martian, a little alien of formidable force created by Chuck Jones, first appeared opposite Bugs Bunny in "Haredevil Hare."

MICHELANGELO. One of the four Teenage Mutant Ninja Turtles. See "Donatello."

MICKEY MOUSE. Beloved Disney mouse whose cohorts included his love, Minnie and friend Goofy, among others. See "Mickey Mouse."

MISS PIGGY. The glamorous pig among the Muppet characters. Miss Piggy was created by a Muppet team member Frank Oz.

MORTIMER. Mortimer Snerd is a dummy brought to life by ventriloquist Edgar Bergen in "The Edgar Bergen and Charlie McCarthy Show" (1936).

MR. BOFFO. A daily comic strip by Cartoonist Joe Martin. Martin was recognized by the Guiness Book of World records as the World's Most Prolific Cartoonist. Other strips include "Willy & Ethel" & "Cats With Hands."

MR. DITHERS. The cranky boss of Dagwood Bumstead in the "Blondie" comics.

MR. GREEN JEANS. Hugh Brannum (1910-1927). Co-star of children's show "Captain Kangaroo" (1955-1984). In his green jeans and jacket, he brought out different animals each day to romp with.

MR. MOOSE. Puppet on "Captain Kangaroo". Wacky Moose (voice of Gus "Cosmo" Allegretti) always tricked the Captain into standing under a shower of ping-pong balls.

MR. POTATO HEAD. A toy manufactured by Hasbro Industries. Originally, plastic facial pieces (ears, eyes, etc.) were supposed to be stuck into a potato to make a face.

MR. SNUFFLEUPAGUS. A "Sesame Street" family of furry elephant-like creatures with a trunk-like appendage called a snuffle. Voice of Jerry Nelson.

MUPPET. A puppet created by Jim Hensen, seen on "Sesame Street."

MUSKRAT. Muskie the Muskrat appeared among the cast of "Deputy Dawg."

NATASHA. Natasha Fatale, a Russian agent and partner of Boris Badenov in "The Bullwinkle Show." Voice of June Foray.

NELL FENWICK. Blonde girlfriend of Dudley Do-Right in "The Bullwinkle Show." Dudley saves Nell from the hands of the villainous Snidley Whiplash.

OLIVE OYL. Popeye's pencil thin girlfriend, created by Elzie Segar.

PEBBLES. Daughter of caveman Fred Flintstone. In true stone-age fashion, Pebbles sported a topknot tied around a bone.

PEPE LE PEW. The antics of an affable French skunk. Voice of Mel Blanc.

PIGPEN. The messiest little boy on the block but still one of the most lovable "Peanuts" characters.

PINK PANTHER. (1964). This lanky-limbed pink animal first appeared in the animated movie "The Pink Panther" by Blake Edwards.

POGO. A possum within the menagerie at Okefenokee Swamp created by Walt Kelly.

POINDEXTER. The little scientist and nephew of The Professor in the "Felix the Cat" cartoon series. Voice of Jack Mercer.

POKEMON. Imported from Japan, the craze for the now famous Pokemon cards have developed into electronic games as well as a full length movie "Pokemon: The Movie 2000." (2000).

POKEY. The pet horse of Gumby on "The Gumby Show." Voice of Art Clokey.

POLLY. A tall, leggy character in a comic strip by Cliff Sterret, depicted old-fashioned parents versus a very fashionable daughter.

PONGO. Father of the stolen puppies in Disney's "The 101 Dalmatians," Pongo and Perdita rescue 99 puppies from the clutches of Cruella DeVil.

POPEYE. (1929). The sailor with the huge forearms who swallows spinach in a single gulp was created by Elzie Segar.

THE PROFESSOR. The outwitted scientist in "Felix the Cat."

PUFNSTUF. H.R. Pufnstuf is a Sid and Marty Krofft puppet.

RAGS. Ragland T. "Rags" Tiger is Crusader Rabbit's pal in the comic adventure "Crusader Rabbit."

RAPHAEL. One of the four Teenage Mutant Ninja Turtles. See "Donatello."

ROCKY. The flying squirrel and his sidekick Bullwinkle battles villains in this series of cartoon cliffhangers "Rocky and His Friends." Voice of June Foray.

SCHROEDER. The musician among the "Peanuts" characters, Schroeder is often seen with his feet to the piano.

SCOOBY-DOO. Adventurous but cowardly sleuth of a Great Dane. Voice of Don Messick. Also, live action movie (2002; 2004).

SIMON. One of the three chipmunks in "The Alvin Show."

SKEEZIX. The main character in the comic strip "Gasoline Alley" by cartoonist Frank O. King. He arrived as an abandoned baby on the doorstep of Walt Wallet on February 14, 1921, and like all the other characters in this strip, has aged in real time.

SMITTY. (1922). Created by Walter Berndt, Smitty was an office boy.

SMURF. A small blue creature who was created by Belgian cartoonist Peyo Culliford.

SNOODLES. Snoodles, a mischievous character, was created by Cyrus Catton Hungerford.

SNOOPY. The almost human dog, is usually found sitting atop his doghouse, in the comic strip "Peanuts" by Charles M. Schulz (1922-2000).

SNUFFY. A furry elephant-like "Sesame Street" creature that lives with his Snuffleupagus family in a cave.

SPEEDY GONZALES. A Mexican mouse who claimed he could run up to 100 miles per hour.

SPLINTER. Kidnapped by the evil Shredder, Splinter the rat ninja master from "Teenage Mutant Ninja Turtles" is saved by these green teen turtles.

TENNESSEE TUXEDO. Tennessee Tuxedo is a penguin and his friend is Walrus Chumley. Together they tackle the conditions at Megalopolis Zoo. Voice of Don Adams.

THEODORE. One of the three chipmunks in "The Alvin Show."

TOM. The cat in the duo "Tom and Jerry." This was the first creation from the cartoon team of Joe Barbera and Bill Hanna.

TOR. See "BC."

TRAMP. The mutt from the other side of town in Disney's "Lady and the Tramp." Tramp turns out to be Lady's hero.

TWINKLE TOES FLINTSTONE. This is Fred Flintstone's nickname when he bowls.

WALDO. A cartoon character from the children's books by Martin Handford "Where's Waldo?" The reader must locate Waldo among a sea of figures and detailed drawings. Waldo, a nerd, wears a knit cap, eyeglasses and striped pullover.

WOODSTOCK. Endearing bird in the "Peanuts" comic strip.

WOODY. The toy cowboy, ever jealous of Buzz Lightyear until they team up to find their way home in the 1995 film "Toy Story." Tom Hanks is the voice of Woody.

YOGI BEAR. As a resident of Jellystone National Park, Yogi and his friend Boo Boo spend their time pilfering picnic baskets and eluding Ranger Smith. Voice of Daws Butler.

YOSEMITE SAM. Created by Friz Freleng, which first appeared opposite Bugs Bunny. Voice of Mel Blanc.

CHAPTER 11

LITERATURE, CHILDREN'S STORIES AND NURSERY RHYMES

LITERATURE

BIFF. Biff is the disillusioned son of salesman Willy Loman in the Arthur Miller Pulitzer Prize winning play "Death of a Salesman" (1949).

BILBO BAGGINS. The hero of J.R.R. Tolkien's "The Hobbit."

BRONTË. Last name of author and sisters, Charlotte "Jane Eyre" (1847); Emily "Wuthering Heights" (1847) and Anne "Agnes Gray" (1847).

BULFINCH. Thomas Bulfinch. (1796-1867). American writer of the "Age of Fable," later known as "Bulfinch's Mythology".

CAPTAIN AHAB. See "Moby Dick."

CHAUCER. Geoffrey Chaucer (1343-1400). Medieval English poet famous for "Canterbury Tales" a group of stories told by pilgrims traveling from London to Canterbury.

DOGBERRY. A character of comic relief in Shakespeare's "Much Ado About Nothing."

FAULKNER. William Faulkner (1897-1962). American writer, whose stories like "The Sound and the Fury," usually took place in the South.

FINIAN. Finian McLonergan is a character who totes gold to America in the E.Y. Harburg's musical "Finian's Rainbow."

FRODO. Character in J.R.R. Tolkien's world, he was adopted by his cousin, Bilbo Baggins at the death of his parents and went on adventures with the Fellowship of the Ring.

FU MANCHU. Created by British writer Sax Rohmer (1883-1959). Fu Manchu is an evil, menacing character that in his torturous ways attempts to rule the world.

GANDALF. A wizard in the novel "The Hobbit" (1937) by J.R.R. Tolkien.

HEMINGWAY. Emest Hemingway (1899-1961). American author and Pulitzer prize winner for "The Old Man and the Sea."

HERCULE POIROT. The Belgian detective in Agatha Christie's (1890-1976) novels.

HOBBIT. A short gentle creature created by J.R.R. Tolkien in "The Hobbit" (1937).

KAFKA. Franz Kafka (1883-1924). Born and lived most of his life in Prague, Czechoslovakia, although he wrote and spoke in German. His works depict his personal struggles.

LONGFELLOW. Henry Wadsworth Longfellow (1807-1882). American poet.

MOBY DICK. (1851). "Moby Dick," the whale in the Herman Melville story. Captain Ahab vows revenge on the whale that took off his leg.

SHERLOCK HOLMES. The private detective made famous by Sir Arthur Conan Doyle (1859-1930).

SIDDHARTHA. Siddhartha "The Buddha" Gautama (c563-483 BC). Siddhartha is the title of the Hermann Hesse novel, a fictionalized account of Buddha's life (1922). Hesse (1877-1962) won the Nobel Prize for literature in 1946. See: "Buddha."

SONNET. A poem with 14 lines, usually on the subject of love.

TARA. Scarlett O'Hara's southern plantation in the novel "Gone With the Wind" (1936), written by Margaret Mitchell.

THOREAU. Henry David Thoreau (1817-1862). American scholar and philosopher lived the simple life on Walden's Pond, wrote "Walden, on Life in the Woods" (1854).

TRUMAN. Truman Capote (1924-1984). American author whose most notable books are "In Cold Blood" and "Breakfast at Tiffany's."

UTOPIA. (1516). Novel written by Sir Thomas More (1478-1535). In it he theorized about the perfect world. More was beheaded by King Henry VIII.

WATSON. Dr. Watson is the assistant to, and foil for "Sherlock Holmes" in the adventures created by Sir Arthur Conan Doyle.

CHILDREN'S STORIES

ANASTASIA. The name of one of the two stepsisters in the fairy tale, Cinderella.

BAMBI. (1923). Written by Austrian, Felix Salten (1869-1945). Bambi is the story of a deer born in a serene German forest and sadly learns of its dangers.

BASHFUL. The shy one of the seven dwarfs from the Grimms' fairy tale. "Snow White and the Seven Dwarfs" was animated by Walt Disney and released in 1937.

CINDERELLA. (1697). Fairy tale by Charles Perrault France. Cinderella is left by the hearth when her stepsisters go off to the ball. Her fairy godmother comes and whisks her off to the ball where she meets her Prince.

DOC. Bespectacled Doc is considered the leader of the seven dwarfs in "Snow White and the Seven Dwarfs" even with his dithering style of speaking.

DRIZELLA. The other mean stepsister to Cinderella in the famous fairy tale.

ELOISE. (1955). Adventures of the precocious little girl who lives at the Plaza Hotel in New York City. Written by Kay Thompson (1902-1998).

GOLDILOCKS. A folktale, presumably by Robert Southey. Goldilocks visits the three bears, eats their porridge and is discovered sleeping in their beds.

HANSEL AND GRETEL. Grimm's fairy tale published in 1812 tells the story of poor parents and their 2 hungry children.

HARRY POTTER. (1998-) The young wizard in training, protagonist of the Harry Potter books who is adopted by Muggles, or non-magical people. Series written by J.K. Rowling.

HOOK. Captain Hook is the menacing pirate in "Peter Pan."

ICHABOD CRANE. The schoolmaster, frightened away by the "Headless Horseman" in Washington Irving's (1783-1859) short story "The Legend of Sleepy Hollow" (1819-1820).

JIMINY CRICKET. Pinocchio's conscience and confidante.

MUGGLES. The non-magical people who populate the Harry Potter books.

PADDINGTON BEAR. The lovable bear found by Mr. and Mrs. Brown at Paddington Station, London.

PETER PAN. The eternally youthful, motherless Peter Pan coaxes Wendy, John and Michael off to Never Never Land.

PIGLET. The small pig resident of the "100 Acre Wood" in A. A. Milne's story. "Piglet" is "Winnie the Pooh's" best friend.

PINOCCHIO. (1881). Pinocchio is a wooden puppet that runs away as soon as his legs and feet are made. His nose grows longer every time he tells a lie. Story written by Carlo Collodi.

PIPPI LONGSTOCKING. (1945). Pippilotta Provisionia Gabesdina Dandeliona, Ephraim's Longstocking daughter, lives alone after her father is lost at sea. Pippi has an eccentric personality and extraordinary strength. Written by Astrid Lindgren.

POOH BEAR. See "Winnie the Pooh."

PUFF. See "Spot."

RAPUNZEL. In this Grimm Brothers' fairy tale, Rapunzel, imprisoned by the witch uses her long yellow hair as a ladder for her prince. Fairy tales written (1812-1815).

RIP VAN WINKLE. (1819-1820). Short story by the American writer, Washington Irving. Rip falls asleep in the Catskill Mountains and wakes up 20 years later, finding the world completely changed.

RUMPELSTILTSKIN. In this Grimm Brothers' fairy tale, a prince comes along and climbs up Rapunzel's long tresses, to rescue her from the witch who banished her.

SPOT. Dick, Jane and their dog Spot had a kitten named Puff, featured in the educational series "Fun with Dick and Jane" (1930's-1960's).

TIGGER. This is "Winnie the Pooh's" gentle tiger companion.

TWEEDLE DEE & TWEEDLE DUM. Characters in Lewis Carroll's (1832-1898) "Through the Looking Glass" (1871).

WENDY. Wendy Darling is coaxed out of her bedroom window and into Never, Never Land by Peter Pan.

WINNIE THE POOH. (1926). A teddy bear named Edward Bear, belonging to author A. A. Milne's son Christopher, became "Winnie the Pooh".

NURSERY RHYMES

GEORGIE PORGIE. This rhyme refers to the teasing antics of the Prince Regent who is to become George IV of England.

HUMPTY DUMPTY. (1803). A "Mother Goose" nursery rhyme, possibly based on an ancient riddle.

JACK AND JILL. A "Mother Goose" rhyme, possibly dating from the 17th century and of Scandinavian origin.

LITTLE BUNNY FOO FOO. A stubborn bunny rabbit who, despite 3 warnings from the Good Fairy, scooped up too many field mice and bopped them on the head, so she turned him into a Goon.

LITTLE BOY BLUE. Who was fast asleep under the haystack.

LITTLE MISS MUFFET. A "Mother Goose" rhyme where Ms. Muffet sat on her tuffet, eating a dairy dish called curds and whey.

OLD KING COLE. The merry old soul. Merry, perhaps because his daughter Helena, after marrying a Roman general, becomes the mother of the Emperor Constantine.

CHAPTER 12

NORTHERN BREEDS

Alaska	Ice Cream	Mr. Freeze	Snowy
Alpine	Icicle	Mrs. Claus	White Fang
Aspen	Igloo	Mush	Wolfy
Bear	Juno; Juneau	Nanook	Yukon
Chilly Willy	Kanook	Nome; Nomi	Zenith
Chinook	Keema; Kima	Panda	
Foxy	Klondike	Popsicle	
Fresca	Koala	Santa	
Frosty	Kodiak	Shasta	
Grizzly	Kona	Slush Puppy	
Ice	Kuma	Snowball	

CHAPTER 13

MILITARY/POLITICAL

ADMIRAL. Commander and chief of a fleet. Naval officer of the highest ranking.

AMBASSADOR. Diplomatic official of the highest rank.

CAPTAIN. A high-ranking military officer.

COLONEL. An officer in the U.S. Army, Air Force or Marine Corps, corresponding to Captain in the U.S. Navy.

COMMANDER. A person who exercises authority; leader, chief officer.

GENERAL. A high-ranking military official.

GOVERNOR. The executive head of a state.

KINGFISH. Huey "Kingfish" Long (1893-1935). Assassinated governor and senator from Louisiana.

LIEUTENANT. A person who holds an office, civil or military in subordination to a superior for whom he acts.

MAJOR. A high-ranking commissioned officer.

MAYOR. Chief executive official of a city, town, or village.

MUGWUMP. Name given to a person during the 1884 U.S. presidential election, who bolted from the Republican Party. "Mugwump" has come to mean an independent acting or neutral person.

OFFICER. A person in authority; police or naval officer.

PATRIOT. A person who loves, supports and defends his or her country.

SERGEANT. A non-commissioned officer.

SOLDIER. A person who serves in an army.

UNCLE SAM. Symbol for the U.S. A grey-haired man dressed in stars, stripes and top hat.

YEOMAN. A Naval petty officer who has chiefly clerical duties.

CHAPTER 14

ANTIHEROES

THOSE WE LOVE TO HATE!

Annihilator

Apocalypse

Barracuda

Beelzebub

Bimbo

Bonehead

Bugsy

Chucky

Commando

Convict

Damien

Demon

Diablo

Dillinger

Ding-a-ling

Ditzi

Dracula

Fatso

Fleabag

Frankenstein

Freddy Kruger

Goblin

Grinch

Hannibal the Cannibal

Hellboy

Hooligan

Ivan the Terrible

Jason

Jaws

Jinx

Killer

Knucklehead

Leatherface

Loch Ness

Lucifer

Lughead

Mad Dog

Mangy

Maniac

Meathead

Misfit

Monster

Nasty Dog

Naughty Dog

Nemesis

Oddball

Outlaw

Pinhead

Radical Dog

Renegade

The Rock

Ruffian

Sable

Satan

Scarface

Scavenger

Scorpion King

Scoundrel

Shark

Snake

Stooge

Tasmanian Devil

Terminator

Turdley

Undertaker

Viper

Warrior

Wench

CHAPTER 15

ETHNIC ORIGINS

BIBLICAL/RELIGIOUS

ANGEL. A celestial being believed by some religions to be a mediator, or the messenger from a deity. Usually classified in a hierarchical manner.

APOCALYPSE. Last book of the New Testament; a prophetic disclosure.

BUDDHA. (c563-483 BC). Founder of Buddhism. His real name was Siddhartha Gautama. Buddha means "Enlightened One." He was born in an area that is now Nepal. Buddha gained enlightenment while sitting under the Bodhi tree.

CORNELIUS. Saint. Pope. Martyred in 253. From Latin meaning "battle horn."

DALAI LAMA. Dalai (High) Lama, the highest spiritual and political leader of the exiled Tibetan people.

DOGMATIC. From the Latin "dogma" which means beliefs, principles. Someone who is Dogmatic is arrogant or overbearing.

ELIJAH. From Hebrew meaning means "My God is Yah." In Jewish tradition, Elijah's return will usher in the Messianic Era.

ENOCH. From the Hebrew meaning "dedicated."

ENOS. From Hebrew meaning "mortal man."

EZEKIEL. From Hebrew meaning "strength of God."

GANDHI. (1869-1948). Mohandas "Mahatma" Karamchand Gandhi was the Indian leader who developed the principle of non-violent civil disobedience. He was assassinated in 1948.

GIDEON. From Hebrew meaning "destroyer."

IGNATIUS. From Latin meaning "fiery."

KRISHNA. Krishna in Hinduism, is the eighth and principal manifestation of Vishnu, a chief deity.

MADONNA. Means "my lady" in Italian, but has come to mean the Virgin Mary in artistic works.

MIRACLE. A supernatural event, usually believed to be the work of God, such as the parting of the Red Sea and Christ's healing of the sick.

MOSES. Leader of the Israelites. Led the Jews out of Egypt to Canaan; declared the Ten Commandments.

PONTIUS PILATE. A Roman governor of Judea, A.D. 26 to 36. Condemned Christ to death, although believing him to be innocent.

SHEBA. From Bathsheba, wife of King David.

SOLOMON. Third king of Israel, son of King David. Ruled Israel from 965 B.C., to his death, possibly 922 B.C.

BRITISH/NOBILITY

BARON. Lower-ranking member of nobility. Middle English, from Old French and of Germanic origin, meaning "man."

BARONESS. A woman holding this title of nobility in her own right, or the wife of a Baron.

BIG BEN. The bell and/or clock in the tower of the Houses of Parliament in London.

BUCKINGHAM. Buckingham Palace is the official residence of the British Monarchy in London.

BUSBY. Tan bearskin hat worn by certain guardsman.

BYRON. Lord George Gordon Byron, English poet 1788-1824. Poetry characterized by romanticism and melancholia.

CHARLES. Prince of Wales, husband/widower of Lady Diana. The name Charles derives from the German word for man.

CHAUNCEY. A nickname from Chancellor from the Middle English meaning "keeper of records."

CHURCHILL. Sir Winston Spencer Leonard. (1874-1965). Prime Minister of the United Kingdom 1940-45 and 1951-55. Churchill is considered a great war leader and the architect of victory of WWII.

COUNTESS. Wife or widow of a count or an earl, or a woman holding the title on her own.

DIANA, PRINCESS OF WALES. (1961-1997). Beloved "Princess Di" was involved in many charitable organizations such as AIDS and eradicating landmines. Also called "Lady Di". See: "Greek/Roman."

DUCHESS. Female leader of a duchy or wife/widow of a Duke.

DUKE. Highest rank of nobility in Britain other than those of the Royal family; male ruler of a Duchy.

EARL. A British nobleman ranking between Marquis and Viscount.

EMPEROR. The ruler of an empire; a species of a butterfly.

EMPRESS. A female ruler or the wife/widow of an emperor.

FERGIE. Sarah Ferguson, the former Duchess of York.

GODIVA. A woman of the 11th Century who agreed to ride naked through Coventry, England if this would relieve the people of a burdensome tax.

KING. A male monarch who holds authority over a country.

LANCELOT. A figure in the legend of King Arthur, one of the most famous of the Knights of the Round Table.

MAJESTY. A royal person or sovereign.

MAJOR. From Latin meaning "great."

NIGEL. A form of the name Neil, from the Latin Nigellus.

PICCADILLY. A familiar area in London, from the Haymarket to Hyde Park Corner.

PRINCE. Non-reigning son of a King or Queen. From Latin word meaning "principal" or "first."

PRINCESS. Daughter of a King or Queen, wife of a prince.

QUEEN. A female ruler or wife of a King.

SQUIRE. In the Middle Ages, a squire was an attendant to a knight with hopes of becoming a knight.

THATCHER. (1925-). Margaret Thatcher was the first woman Prime Minister of Great Britain (1979-1990).

TRIFLE. A scrumptious dessert of English origin made with ladyfingers, jam, sherry, custard, whipped cream and almonds.

VISCOUNT. A nobleman ranking between an earl and a baron.

CHINESE

CHAN. A celebrated king of Cambodia who reigned between 1516-1566.

CHIN CHIN. Means "to your health."

CHINA. The People's Republic of China, has an estimated one billion people.

CHOPSTICKS. A pair of stick-type utensils used for eating in Asian cultures.

CONFUCIUS. A Chinese philosopher, Confucius is Latin for "Master Kong."

FENG SHUI. Means "Wind and Water." Ancient Chinese practice of physical placement.

GENGHIS KHAN. (c1167-1227). Means "Universal Ruler," he organized Mongol tribes and became leader of an Empire that stretched from Eastern Europe to the Sea of Japan.

I CHING. "I Ching" or the Book of Changes, is one of the five classics of ancient Chinese literary works, consisting of 64 hexagrams and used to explain the unknown.

KUNG FU. A Chinese form of self-defense using circular movements.

LING LING. A female giant Panda given to the U.S. by China in 1972 following Richard Nixon's trip to China.

MAH JONG. A Chinese game played with 4 people using domino-like tiles with symbols.

MAO. Mao Tse-Tung (1893-1976). A Marxist and founder of the Chinese Communist Party and leader of the People's Republic.

MEI XIANG. Along with her companion Tian Tian, these two pandas arrived from China on December 6, 2000 to live at the Washington Zoo. "Mei Xiang" means beautiful fragrance.

MING. Ming dynasty was established in China at Nanking in 1368 by Chu Yuan-Chang, a commoner who came to be known as the Hung Wu Emperor.

PANDA. The Giant Panda is actually a member of the raccoon family and is found in Tibet and Western China and feeds on bamboo.

TANG. Tang Dynasty (618-907) centralized the government of China.

TIAN TIAN. Means more and more. One of a pair of pandas. See "Mei Xiang."

YIN AND YANG. In Chinese philosophy, Yin is the feminine passive force of nature as opposed to the masculine active force of nature, the Yang.

F R E N C H

BABETTE. A French form of the name Elizabeth.

BIJOU. Jewel; gem.

BISTRO. A small restaurant in France where wine is served.

BRIE. A soft cheese from the Brie region of France.

CAVIAR. Black caviar, a delicacy is black or gray fish eggs from the sturgeon and red caviar is from the roe of the salmon.

CHABLIS. A greenish-golden wine from an area of the village of Chablis, in the Burgundy region of France.

CHALET. French word meaning "little castle." These wooden houses are typically found in the region of the Alps.

CHAMOIS. An animal in the goat family whose leather has been used to make chamois leather cloths.

CHAMPAGNE. A sparkling white wine from a region in France that at one time was the province of Champagne.

CHANEL. (1883-1971). French fashion designer whose real name is Gabrielle Bonheur Chanel, known as "Coco".

CHARDONNAY. A white grape used in the making of Chardonnay wine.

CHARLEMAGNE. (742-814). Charles the Great, Charles I, King of France (768-814), Emperor of the Holy Roman Empire.

CHERIE. A French word meaning "dearest or darling."

CHIFFON. A sheer, light fabric from the French "chiffe," a rag or piece of cloth.

DIJON. A city in France known for its mustard and a liqueur called Cassis.

FABERGÉ. Carl Fabergé (1846-1920). His jeweled Easter eggs are his hallmark.

FRENCHY. Bestowed as a nickname on someone of a French background.

GIGI. Shortened form of any of the feminine forms of George: Georgine, Georgette, Georgiana and Georgia.

JACQUES. The French name for James.

JULIETTE. A form of the name Julia.

LOUPGAROU. Meaning "werewolf." Loup means "wolf."

MADAME BOVARY. (1857). The adulterous character and title of French author Gustave Flaubert's (1821-1880) first published novel.

MADEMOISELLE. Miss, young lady.

MARDI GRAS. French term meaning "Fat Tuesday" or "Shrove Tuesday," the day before the beginning of Lent.

MERCI. Mercy, discretion, thank you.

MONIQUE. French name for Monica.

MONSIEUR. My lord, sir, gentleman.

NAPOLÉON. Napoléon Bonaparte (1769-1821). Napoléon I, was a great military leader. Crowned himself Emperor of the French (1804).

NOUBA. A group of Algerian or Moroccan regiments. A showy group; a noisy feast.

PIERRE. French version of Peter.

POTPOURRI. A fragrant mixture of dried flower petals.

ROUGE. Red.

ROULETTE. A casino game of chance played with a rotating wheel and a small plastic ball.

SHALIMAR. A perfume created in 1925 by Jacques Guerlain is composed of sandalwood, ambergris, musk and civet.

SOLEIL. Sun; sunshine.

TARTUFFE. A hypocrite in the comedy of the same name by French playwright, Moliere (1622-1673).

TUTU. A ballerina's short, bouffant skirt.

VOLTAIRE. François Marie Arouet. (1694-1778). Voltaire's intelligence, wit and style made him one of France's greatest writers and philosophers.

GERMANIC LANGUAGES
(GERMAN, AUSTRIAN, DANISH AND DUTCH)

ADOLPH. Teutonic for "noble helper" or "noble wolf."

AUTOBAHN. Superhighway in Germany.

BISMARCK. Otto Eduard Leopold von Bismarck (1815-1898). First Chancellor of the German Empire.

DIETRICH. From the Teutonic name Theodoric, meaning "people's rule." German form of Derek.

FRANZ. German form of Francis which means "a free man" in Middle English.

FRAULEIN. Young lady.

FRITZ. German form of Frederick, from the Teutonic "peaceful ruler."

GESELLE. A name of German origin meaning "assistant."

GRETA. A form of Margaret used in Sweden.

GRETCHEN. German form of Margaret, from Greek meaning "pearl."

GRETEL. A version of Gretchen which is a German form of Margaret.

GUNNAR. A Scandinavian name from Old Norse meaning "war."

HANS. A form of John used by Dutch, German and Swedes. John is from the Hebrew meaning "God is gracious."

HANSEL. Bavarian form of John.

HEIDE. Swiss meaning "Little Miss." Abbreviation of Adelheid.

HELGA. Anglo-Saxon meaning "Holy."

HELMUT. From the Teutonic meaning "to cover," as a helmet covers the head.

INGRID. Scandinavian variation of Inga. In Norse mythology, "Ing" is the god of fertility and peace.

KAISER. German meaning "emperor." From the Latin Caesar.

LIEBCHEN. Sweetheart.

LUTHER. A version of Lothar from the Teutonic for "noted warrior."

MATA HARI. (1876-1917). Gertrud Margaretha Zelle was a Dutch dancer who was executed as a spy in WWI.

NEANDERTHAL. Species of man that lived during the late Pleistocene period. The Neanderthal is a valley near Dusseldorf, Germany where in 1856 evidence of the Neanderthal Man was found.

NIETZSCHE. Friedreich Wilhelm Nietzsche (1844-1900). German philosopher.

OTTO. Teutonic for "prosperous."

ROMMEL. Erwin Rommel (1891-1944). German field marshal of World War II, nicknamed "The Desert Fox."

SCHATZIE. "Sweetheart."

SCHNAPPS. A strong dry liqueur such as a "aquavit" or "kirsch."

SIEGFRIED. From the Teutonic meaning "victorious peace."

SIGMUND. Teutonic for "protecting conqueror."

THOR. God of Thunder and War in Norse Mythology.

VAN GOGH. Vincent (1853-1890). Dutch impressionist painter who cut off his ear.

ZSA ZSA. Shortened form of the Hungarian name for Susan, Zsusanna.

GREEK / ROMAN

ACHILLES. The hero of "The Iliad" by Homer.

ADONIS. In Greek mythology, a gorgeous youth loved by Aphrodite.

AGAPE. Greek word for love.

AJAX. A warrior in Greek mythology who fought against Troy.

APHRODITE. The Goddess of love in Greek mythology, she was one of the twelve Olympian Gods.

ARISTOTLE. A Greek philosopher who wrote about logic, philosophy, ethics, politics and poetics; pupil of Plato.

ATHENA. Born out of the head of Zeus. One of the twelve Olympian Gods. The Goddess of wisdom.

CALIGULA. Emperor of Rome 12-41 A.D. Also known as Gaius Caesar, he was tyrannical and ultimately assassinated.

CYCLOPS. A member of a family of giants who have a single eye in the middle of their forehead.

DIDO. The Queen of Carthage, whose love for Aeneas caused her to throw herself on a funeral pyre at his parting.

DIMITRI. From the Greek goddess Demeter, goddess of agriculture.

ELECTRA. Daughter of Agamemnon and Clytemnestra, she convinces her brother to murder their mother in reprisal for the murder of Agamemnon by Clytemnestra's lover.

EROS. The God of love in Greek mythology, youngest of the gods. Identified with wings and arrows and called Cupid by the Romans.

FETA. A crumbly white cheese with a sharp salty taste made from goat or sheep's milk.

FILO/PHYLLO. Meaning "leaf," this Greek pastry dough is used in baking.

GLADIATOR. A combatant who was trained to entertain the public in the Roman arena by engaging in combat.

GRIFFIN. In Greek mythology, a beast with the body of a lion and the head and wings of an eagle.

HELIOS. Sun God in Greek mythology, identified as driver of a chariot.

HERCULES. Mythological figure of enormous strength.

ISIS. In Egyptian mythology, the Goddess of fertility.

MEDEA. A princess who assisted Jason in obtaining the Golden Fleece.

NEPTUNE. According to Roman mythology, this is the God of the sea.

NIKE. Greek Goddess of victory.

OEDIPUS. In Greek mythology, he killed his father, King Laius of Thebes, and married his mother, Jocasta.

OLYMPIA. An area where the original Olympic games were held.

OMEGA. Last letter of the Greek alphabet as opposed to the first letter, Alpha.

ORION. In Greek mythology identified as a hunter, son of Poseidon.

PANDORA. According to Greek mythology, the first woman. She opened a box out of curiosity and unleashed all the evils of the world.

PLATO. Greek philosopher, pupil of Socrates and founder of the Academy where Aristotle studied.

PYGMALION. In Greek mythology, a king of Cyprus who carved a statue of a woman and fell in love with her.

SPARTACUS. Leader of the revolt against Rome 73-71 B.C.

THEO. From Greek word "theos" meaning "God."

TITAN. In Greek mythology, children of Uranus and Gaea, considered to be giant beings.

VENUS. In Roman mythology, the Goddess of love; mother of Cupid.

VESTA. Goddess who protects her home.

XENO. From Greek word "Xenos," meaning "stranger."

YANNI. See "Musicians."

ZEUS. Identified in Greek mythology as a God of the sky. One of twelve Olympian Gods.

ZORBA. Alexis Zorba is the exhilarating hero of the novel "Zorba the Greek" by Nikos Kazantzakis.

HAWAIIAN

AHI. AH-hee. "Fire."

AKUA. uh-KOO-uh. "God," "spirit," idol."

HONUA. hoh-NOO-uh. "Earth."

IPO. EE-poh. "Sweetheart."

KANANI. Kuh-NAH-nee. "The pretty one."

KEKOA. Keh-KOH-uh. "The courageous one."

LANI. LAH-nee. "Sky, heaven."

LUANA. Loo-AH-nuh. "Enjoyment."

MAKAMAKA. Mah-kuh-Mah-kuh. "Friend."

MAKANI. Muh-KAH-nee. "Wind."

MANU. MAH-noo. "Bird."

MOI. MOH-EE. "King."

PO. POH. "Night."

PUA. POO-uh. "Flower.

HEBREW / YIDDISH

ALIYAH. Means "going up." One can make aliyah to Israel (immigrate), or up to the bima (the altar in a synagogue) to recite blessings.

BAGEL. A hard round doughnut-shaped bread. From the German word "beugel" meaning "round bread."

BLINTZ. A pancake folded over a filling of fruit or cheese mixture, fried and topped with sour cream.

BOYCHIK. A little boy.

BUBELE. BUB-ah-lah. Darling grandchild.

DYBBUK. A wandering soul in need of a human body to control, it must be exorcised in order to find rest.

GONIF. Yiddish for thief or clever person.

KASHA. Buckwheat groats; cereal.

KIBITZER. Someone who chats or converses; jokes.

KLUTZ. Clumsy person.

LATKE. LAT-kah. Grated potato pancake.

MAISIE. A form of Miriam from the Hebrew meaning "sea of sorrow."

MAVEN. Yiddish for expert. From Hebrew "mevin," meaning "understanding,"

MAZEL. Luck.

MENSCH. A good person.

MESHUGGE. Crazy, insane.

NOSH. A snack, from German "naschen," to nibble.

NUDGH. Nuhdje. To pester, to nag.

NUDNIK. A bore, a pest.

SCHMUTZ. Dirt; smut.

SHALOM. Hebrew for Solomon (son of David), meaning peace."

SHIKSA. Non-Jewish woman.

SHNORRER. A freeloader or moocher.

YENTA. A female busybody.

IRISH

BANSHEE. In Irish folklore, a female spirit who wails outside a house and portends a death.

BLARNEY. Flattery. If one kisses the Blarney Stone in Ireland, they would come away with the skill of flattery.

CLANCY. Son of Flannchadh (a ruddy warrior).

COSTELLO. Son of Oisdealbh; fawn-like.

DUFFY. From the County Monaghan, Duffy is the most popular family name. It derives from O'Dubhthaigh, which means descendant of Dubhthach, the black one.

GRANUAILE. In Irish folklore she is Queen of the Sea.

HOULIHAN. English form of the Gaelic O'hUallachgn, from the word uallach, meaning "proud."

LEPRECHAUN. In Irish folklore, an elf knowing the whereabouts of hidden treasure.

MEGAN. The strong (Teutonic origin).

MURPHY. Sea warrior.

PADDY. Irish form of Patrick. From Latin meaning "noble one."

QUINN. The wise.

SHAMROCK. Symbol of Ireland, a stem with three leaflets.

SWEENY. Son of a peaceful person.

ITALIAN

AMARETTO. An almond-flavored liqueur. Comes from the word amaro meaning "bitter."

BELLA. Italian word for beautiful from the Latin Bellus, meaning "pretty."

BIANCA. Italian female name meaning "white."

CAPPUCCINO. A coffee beverage prepared by combining steamed milk with espresso coffee.

COLUMBUS. Christopher Columbus (1451-1506). Italian navigator who sailed under the flag of Spain in search of the "New World."

COSMO. From the Greek word "kosmos" meaning "order and universe."

DANTE. Dante Alighieri (1265-1321). An Italian poet who wrote "Divine Comedy."

DOLCE. Sweet, gentle.

FELLINI. Federico Fellini (1920-1993). Oscar-winning Italian filmmaker.

GALILEO. Galilei Galileo (1564-1642). Astronomer, mathematician, physicist. Developed the astronomical telescope.

GUIDO. Italian form of Guy.

LIDO. An island off the coast of Italy, near Venice.

LIRA. Monetary unit of Italy, equal to 100 centesimi.

LUIGI. Italian form of the French name Louis which comes from the Teutonic Hlodwig, meaning "famous war."

MACARONI. Tube-shaped pasta made of dough from flour and water.

MUSSOLINI. Benito Mussolini (1883-1945). Dictator of Italy from (1924 to 1943).

NERO. Claudius Caesar Drusus Germanicus Nero. (37-68 AD). Roman Emperor from 54 to 68 A.D.

PACE. Pah-chay. Peace, tranquility.

PAISANO. Fellow countryman; slang usage for buddy, pal.

PASTA. Noodles made from dough of flour and water.

PESTO. Crushed, pounded; a sauce made from basil, pine nuts and olive oil.

POMPEII. A city, south of Naples, Italy, destroyed by an eruption of Mount Vesuvius in 79 A.D.

TORTELLINI. Stuffed pasta, supposedly made in the shape of Venus' navel.

VALENTINO. Rudolph Valentino (1895-1926). Italian silent film star that was known as "The Great Lover."

J A P A N E S E

AIBO. Pal.

ASIMO. Honda Motors' humanoid robot who rang the opening bell of the New York Stock Exchange on February 15, 2002.

BANZAI. Patriotic shout used among combat troops.

BONSAI. Japanese art of cultivating miniature or dwarf trees.

GINZU. A Ginzu knife is an indestructible instrument whose cutting feats have been depicted in commercials.

HAIKU. A Japanese form of poetry usually celebrating nature.

HIBACHI. Japanese-style cooking grill.

HONCHO. Person in charge.

JUDO. A sport developed from jujitsu that emphasizes the use of quick movement and leverage to throw an opponent.

KAMIKAZE. Literal meaning is "divine wind," though generally known as a suicide plane or pilot.

KIMONO. A loose, wide-sleeved satin or silk robe fastened at the waist with a wide sash.

KYOTO. A major city in Japan on the island of Honshu. Capital of Japan from 794-1868.

MIKA. New moon (Japanese female name).

MIKO. A fortune teller.

OKI. Big dog.

OSO. A bear.

SAKANA. Sa-ka-nah. Means fish.

SAKE. An alcoholic drink made from fermented rice.

SAMURAI. These swordsman were the hereditary warrior class of feudal Japan who placed honor above life.

SHINGO. See "Sports."

SHOGUN. Titles given to military leaders that controlled Japan from (1192 to 1867).

SUKI. Beloved (Japanese female name).

SUSHI. Boiled rice, wrapped seaweed seasoned with vinegar and topped with raw fish, fish eggs, and vegetables.

TENGU. God of Mischief.

TOFU. A type of food made from soybean curd and of the consistency of custard.

TORA. Tiger

YOKI. Good, fine.

YOKO. Positive child or female principle.

YOSHI. Female name meaning "happy," "good," "fine".

YUKI. Male or Female name meaning "snow."

MIDDLE EASTERN

ALADDIN. Arabic for "height of faith."

ALI. Form of Allah. Arabic for "God" as in Ali Baba in "The Arabian Nights."

ALLAH. Arabic for "God."

CLEOPATRA. (69-30 B.C.). Queen of Egypt; Greek for "fame of her father."

FALAFEL. Crushed garbanzo and fava beans, bourghool, split peas, mixed with exotic natural spices and deep-fried in oil.

MOHAMMED. From Arabic meaning "praised". The Prophet of Islam.

PHARAOH. A ruler of ancient Egypt.

PITA. A Middle-Eastern flat, round pocket bread.

SULTAN. A sovereign leader of a Muslim state.

TAHINA. Tahina or sesame paste, is an emulsion of sesame seeds and oil.

NATIVE AMERICANS

APACHE. Tribe of Native Americans occupying American Southwest and Northern Mexico.

CHEROKEE. Tribe of Native Americans originally occupying North Carolina and Northern Georgia, now settled in Oklahoma.

CHEYENNE. Native Americans originally settled in central Minnesota and North and South Dakota, now in Montana and Oklahoma.

CHIEF. Leader of an Native American nation or tribe.

CHINOOK. Native Americans originally within the Columbia River Basin in Oregon.

COMANCHE. Native Americans originally occupying western plains from Wyoming to Texas, now settled in Oklahoma.

GERONIMO. Chief of the Apaches, 1829-1909.

HOPI. A group of Native Americans settled in northeastern Arizona.

KEMOSABE. This is the term used by Tonto to address his companion, The Lone Ranger in the T.V. series "The Lone Ranger." In the Potawatomi language it means "trusty scout."

NAVAJO. A group of Native Americans occupying New Mexico, Arizona and Utah.

SACAJEWEA. (c1790-1812?). Shoshone guide with the Lewis and Clark expedition. She was the wife of interpreter, Toussaint Charbonneau.

SASQUATCH. A large, hairy primate comparable to the Abominable Snowman or the Siberian Almas. Sasquatch is from the word se'sxac meaning "wild men" in the Salish language of an Native American tribe.

SIOUX. Group of Northern Native Americans who originally occupied Great Plains in the Dakotas, Minnesota and Nebraska.

TOTEM. An object (as an animal or plant) serving as the emblem of a family or clan, and often as a reminder of its ancestry.

WAMPUM. "Money."

WIGWAM. Once a home of the Northeast Native Americans. This oval shaped structure that was made sturdy from bent tree poles and covered with beds of grass in the summer, and bark and animal skins in the winter.

ZUNI. Native Americans occupying western New Mexico.

S L A V I C   L A N G U A G E S
(RUSSIAN, POLISH, CZECH)

BARYSHNIKOV, MIKHAIL. (1948). Russian ballet dancer actor who defected Canada, then to the United States in 1974, joining the American Ballet Theatre.

BORIS. Slavic for "fighting warrior."

COMRADE. In Russia, comrade is usually referred to a fellow member of the Communist Party.

CZAR. Title of former rulers of Russia.

CZARINA. Female of Czar.

GODUNOV. Alexander Godunov (1949-1995). Russian ballet dancer/actor who defected to the West in 1979, during the Bolshoi Ballet's American tour.

GORBY. Nickname for Mikhail Gorbachev (1931-). Became General Secretary of the Soviet Communist Party in 1985. He promoted political and economic reform. Became President of the USSR in 1990, resigned in 1991.

IVAN. Russian version of John, meaning "grace."

IVAN THE TERRIBLE. (1533-1584). Crowned the first Czar of all Russia in 1547, he was a ruthless and paranoid ruler.

IVANA. Feminine form of Ivan, the Russian form of John, from the Hebrew meaning, "God is gracious."

KATARINA. A variation of Katherine, from Greek meaning "pure."

KIELBASA. A smoked, garlic seasoned pork Polish sausage.

MISHKA. Russian form of Michael.

NADIA. Slavic for "hope."

NATASHA. Russian pet name for Natalia.

NIJINSKY. Vaslav Najinsky (1890-1950). Legendary Russian ballet dancer.

NUREYEV. Rudolf Nureyev (1938-1993). Ballet dancer and choreographer, born in Russia, defected in 1961 to the West.

ODESSA. A seaport on the southwestern coast of the Ukraine, on the Black Sea. Originally settled in 800 B.C. by Greeks.

OKSANA. Oksana Bauil (1977-). This Ukrakainian born figure skater rose from humble beginnings to win the Gold Medal in the 1994 Winter Olympics.

PAVLOV. Ivan Petrovich Pavlov (1849-1936). Russian physiologist known for his work with dogs in the discovery of the conditioned reflex.

POLKA. An Eastern European folk dance in 2/4 time that became very popular in the 1830's and 1840's.

RASPUTIN. Gregory Rasputin (1869-1916). The powerful monk who gained prominence in the court of Nicholas and Alexandra.

RUBLE. Basic monetary unit of Russia, equal to 100 kopecks.

SPUTNIK. Means "traveling companion" in Russian. The satellite project launched by Soviets in 1957 to test conditions of space.

STOLI. Stolichnaya. Russian vodka.

STRAVINSKY. Igor Stravinsky. See "Musicians."

TITO. Josip Broz (1892-1980). Ruler of Yugoslavia after World War II.

TOLSTOY. Leo Nikolaevich Tolstoy (1828-1910). Russian writer of the classic "War and Peace."

VLADE. Slavic for "world prince."

ZIMA. Means "winter."

S P A N I S H / L A T I N

AMIGO. Friend.

BAMBA. "La Bamba" Mexican dance; fluke.

BLANCA. Spanish form of Blanch from the Old French, meaning "white, fair skinned."

BONITA. Pretty.

BURRITO. A young donkey or a rolled and filled tortilla.

CHICO. A nickname for Charles which means "strong."

CHILI. Chile or chili pepper. A pepper from the species capsicum, used for cooking.

CHIQUITA/CHIQUITO. Small, tiny.

CISCO. Shortened form of Francisco, from Francis meaning "free man."

CORONA. Spanish surname from the Latin word for crown.

DAIQUIRI. A cocktail of rum, lime juice and sugar mixed with ice. Named after a town in Cuba.

FELIZ. Portuguese form of Felix from the Latin meaning "happy."

FERNANDO. From Ferdinand, which is originally of Gothic Origin. In Spain it became Fernando.

FIESTA. Party, celebration or festival.

GATO. A tomcat, alley cat or stray. A cat.

GORDO/GORDA. Fat.

HOMBRE. Man.

LIMA. A lime, or the capital of Peru.

LOCO. Crazy, mad or insane.

LUPE. Short for Guadalupe. Means "Crusher of the Stone Serpent," as a description of the way the Virgin Mary turned the Aztec Indians away from the worship of their stone snake idol.

MAMBO. A fast-paced Caribbean or Latin American ballroom dance similar to Rumba and Cha Cha.

MARGARITA. Derivation of the name Margaret from the Greek "margaretes" meaning "pearl." Also a drink mixed with Tequila.

MATADOR. A bullfighter.

MESCAL. Intoxicating beverage from juice of agave plants.

MUCHACHA/MUCHACHO. Girl or boy.

NEGRITA. Young black girl.

NIÑA/NIÑO. Young/small girl or boy.

PABLO. Spanish form of Paul.

PACO. Spanish for Frank or Francis.

PALOMA. Spanish female name for "dove."

PANAMA. A republic in Central America.

PANCHO. Article of clothing; a cone-like wrap with no sleeves on the neckline.

PEDRO. Spanish form of the name Peter.

PEPE. Spanish form of the Italian Guiseppe (Joseph).

PERRO. Spanish for "dog."

PESO. A monetary unit of countries such as Mexico, Chile, Colombia, Cuba, and the Dominican Republic.

PICASSO. Spanish artist Pablo Picasso (1881-1973).

PONCE. Spanish surname from the Latin word "pontuis" meaning "sailor."

POQUITO. A little bit.

SALSA. Contemporary Latin American music or ballroom dance originating of Cuban and Mexican rhythms.

SAMBA. Ballroom dance of Brazilian-African origin.

SIESTA. Afternoon nap.

TACO. A soft or crisp tortilla filled with beef, chicken, or fish, accented with a tangy sauce (salsa).

TANGO. A Latin American ballroom dance characterized with pointed movements and dramatic dips.

TEQUILA. Mexican beverage created by the Spaniards in the 1500's, from the blue agave plant. Tequila is the state in Mexico where this plant is found.

TITO. Spanish form of Titus from the Greek "of the giants."

TORO. Bull.

XUXA. (1963-). Born Maria da Graca Meneghel. Xuxa (pronounced shu sha) is a very popular, highly successful hostess of a Brazilian children's television show.

CHAPTER 16

COLORFUL PETS

Beige

Buttercup	Fawn	Pearl	Tawny
Butterscotch	Honey	Putty	Toffee
Caramel	Khaki	Sandy	Tumbleweed
Cream Puff	Opal	Taffy	

Black

Batman	Darkman	Nebula	Pygmy
Black Cat	Dracula	Negra	Raven
Blackberry	Ebony	Negrita	Shadow
Blackhawk	Eight Ball	Nimbus	Spade
Blackie	Elvira	Noche	Spook
Blackjack	Jet	Onyx	Tar Baby
Blacksmith	Licorice	Panther	Tornado
Blackwell	Limo	Pepper	Vampire / Vampirella
Blackstreet	Magic	Phantom	
Caviar	Midnight	Puck	
Coal	Morticia		

Black & White

Chex	Ling Ling	Penguin	Tux
Domino	Oreo	Tuxedo	

NAME THAT PET!

Blue

Blue	Bluegrass	Misty
Bluebell	Indigo	Periwinkle

Brown

Autumn	Chip	Kahlúa	Sequoia
Bosco	Coco	Kong	Sienna
Brindle	Cognac	Leroy Brown	Spice
Brown Sugar	Devil Dog	Mocha	Tootsie Roll
Brownie	Fudge	Mahogany	Truffles
Bruno	Ginger	Molasses	Turdley
Cappuccino	Hershey	Pepsi	
Carob	Hickory	Pretzel	
Chestnut	Java	Sable	

Gold

Amber	Goldfinger	Goldilocks	Midas
Gilda	Goldie	Marigold	Nugget

Green

Alley Gator	Froggy	Leprechaun	Pea Pod
Basil	Kelly	Margarita	Ribbit
Chartreuse	Kermit	Money	Shamrock
Clover	Kiwi	Olive	Sweet Pea

COLORFUL PETS

Grey

Ash; Ashes	Cinder	Smokey
Ashley	Greystoke	Smudge

Multi

Brindle	Confetti	Rainbow
Calico	Mix	

Orange

Cheddar	Nutmeg	Sandy	Topaz
Colby	Papaya	Tang	
Curry	Pumpkin	Tangerina	

Purple

Lilac	Orchid	Violet

Red / Pink

Apples	Crimson	Pink Panther	Rosebud
Big Red	Cupid	Pinky	Rouge
Brandy	Diablo	Punch	Ruby
Carrot Top	Fire	Red	Scarlet
Cayenne	Flame	Red Baron	Valentine
Cherry	Henna	Red Devil	
Cinnamon	Magenta	Rojo	
Clay	Pepto	Rose; Rosie	

Silver

Dolomite	Metallica	Silverado	Sterling
Mercury	Silver	Slinky	Tin Man

White

Ajax	Diamond	Mummy	Spook (y)
Alabaster	Frosty	Popcorn	Sugar
Albino	Ivory	Snow White	White Fang
Bianca	Marshmallow	Snowball	Whitey
Blanca (o)	Mayo	Snowflake	
Casper	Moon	Snowy	

Yellow

Blondie	Macaroni	Summer	Sunset
Cornflake	Noodles	Sunburst	Sunshine
Dijon	Old Yeller	Sunni	Topaz
Flaxen	Pasta	Sunrise	Twinkie

CHAPTER 17

TRANSPORTATION

TRAINS, PLANES, AUTOMOBILES AND MORE!

AERO. A compact passenger car manufacturer by Willys in 1953.

ALFA ROMERO. Italian Sports Car developed by Ugo Stella in 1909.

ASTON MARTIN. Lionel Martin and Robert Bamford built the first Aston Martin in 1914 in England.

AUDI. German engineered vehicle created by August Horch in 1901.

BARRACUDA. A Plymouth fastback, hardtop coupe (1965).

BEEMER. BMW. Bavarian Motor Works. First car built was the BMW Wartburg (1928).

BEETLE. The VW people's car, the Beetle was Germany's bug design of 1938.

BENTLEY. British sports car (1920-) bought by Rolls Royce in 1931.

BLAZER. A 5-door or 3-door vehicle with either 2-wheel or 4-wheel drive, manufactured by Chevrolet.

BOXCAR. A completely enclosed freight car.

BOXTER. Type of Porche.

NAME THAT PET!

BRONCO. This 4 wheel-drive vehicle was added to the Ford lineup in 1966.

CABOOSE. Last car on a train, toot toot!

CAPRICE. A model in the Chevrolet lineup.

CHASSIS. The steel frame that holds the body and motor of an automobile.

CHEROKEE. A very popular vehicle manufactured by Jeep, introduced in 1984 with 4-wheel drive and off-road capabilities.

CHEVY. Racecar driver Louis Chevrolet and engineer Etienne Planche produced prototypes of this American car in 1911.

CHOO CHOO. Kiddie language for railroad train.

CHOPPER. Slang for helicopter or a motorcycle.

COUGAR. A sporty car by Mercury which at its inception (1967) rivaled the Ford Mustang.

DUSTER. A semi-fastback coupe by Chevrolet appeared in 1970.

EDSEL. A Ford disappointment (1958-1960).

FERRARI. An Italian sports car by Enzo Ferrari (1946-).

FREEWAY. A highway free of traffic lights, intersections and tolls.

HOT ROD. An automobile especially adapted for racing at accelerated speeds.

ISUZU. Japanese car from Isuzu of Tokyo since 1953.

JAGUAR. Jaguar Cars, Ltd. Founded by William Lyons in 1945.

JETTA. A small sedan by Volkswagen.

JUSTY. A small, reliable car manufactured by Subaru.

LIMO. Short for limousine, a large multi-passenger vehicle.

LOTUS. A sports car engineered in England by Anthony Colin Bruce Chapman.

LYNX. Mercury introduced as a small 3-door hatchback sedan in 1981.

MG. MG stands for "Morris Garages" where founder Cecil Kimber worked as manager when the first MG's were built in 1923.

MERCEDES. German motorcar produced by Emile Jellinek and Wilhelm Mayback in 1901.

ORVILLE. Orville Wright (1871-1948). Orville, along with his brother Wilbur, invented, built and flew the first power-driven, flight machine.

PACER. A subcompact that was built by American Motors Cars in 1975.

PEUGEOT. Originally a steam car built by Armond Peugeot in France (1889).

PORSCHE. Designed by Ferdinand Porsche (1875-1951), first in Austria and then in Germany. They are known for speed, power and longevity.

ROCKET. A projectile-like device or missile.

ROVER. This British car was designed by Edmund Lewis (1904).

SCAMP. A hardtop Mercury compact introduced in the 70's.

SCHOONER. A large sailboat with two masts, a foresail, a mainsail and one or more jibs.

SCOOTER. A footboard for kids with wheels at both ends and a steering column.

SHELBY. Shelby Cobras and Shelby GT's were modifications of Mustangs by racecar driver Carroll Shelby (1962-1970).

SIDEKICK. A sport utility, 2-wheel or 4-wheel drive vehicle manufactured by Suzuki.

STORM. GEO Storm is a sporty 3-door coupe.

SUBARU. Japanese car by Juji Sangyo (1958).

SUZUKI. Japanese car by Suzuki Shokkuki Seisakusho (1955).

TANK. Armored vehicle mounted with guns, used in combat.

TAXI. A for-hire auto that calculates fares.

TITANIC. The doomed oceanliner that sank on her maiden voyage, April 14, 1912.

TRAM. An open train-like vehicle used as a shuttle to transport passengers for a short distance.

TRUCKER. A truck driver.

TURBO. Pertains to being driven by a turbine engine.

VETTE. This sportscar, the Chevrolet Corvette, appeared with a fiberglass body (1953).

ZAPPY. Electrical-powered scooter. With a speed of up to 13 miles per hour, you can park your car anywhere and still get to the show on time!

CHAPTER 18

SPORTS

ALI. Mohammad Ali. Born Cassius Clay (1942-). "The Greatest" is a three time heavyweight champion boxer.

ALZADO. Lyle Alzado (1949-1992). Former NFL defensive end and Los Angeles Raiders football star.

BABE. George Herman "Babe" Ruth (1895-1968). Originally a pitcher for the Boston Red Sox, his greatest achievements were for hitting 60 home runs (1927) and 714 hits during his lifetime.

BAT BOY/BAT GIRL. A kid who takes care of bats and other equipment in baseball.

B-BALL. Nickname for Basketball.

BLACK HAWK. Chicago Black Hawks, an NHL hockey team.

BLITZ. In football, defensive players charge a quarterback, as soon as the ball is snapped, in order to sack him.

BOGEY. In golf, a score of one over par on a hole.

BOOG. John Wesley "Boog" Powell. (1941-). First baseman for the Baltimore Orioles. Went on to open a concession stand at Camden Yards, write a BBQ cookbook and do T.V. commercials.

BOOMER. Norman Julius "Boomer" Esiason (1961-). Quarterback for the Cincinnati Bengals.

BOOMERANG. A weapon used by Australian Aborigines with a curved design that allows the weapon to return to thrower.

BRONCO. AFL Denver Broncos' home is Mile High Stadium.

BRUCE LEE. (1941-1973). Martial arts expert/actor.

BRUIN. The Bruins are the UCLA football team, cross-town rival of University of Southern California Trojans, and both are contenders for the Rose Bowl.

BULL. Chicago Bulls championship basketball team led by superstar Michael Jordan.

BULLET. Washington Bullets, a basketball team (NBA).

BULL'S EYE. The very center circle on a target, as in archery.

BUTKUS. Dick Butkus (1942-). Football player for Chicago Bears (1965-1973).

CASEY. Charles Dillon "Casey" Stengel (1890-1975). Hall of Fame baseball player, manager and coach.

CATCHER. A player on a baseball team who stands behind home plate and catches pitches.

CATFISH. Jim "Catfish" Hunter (1946-1999). Hall of Fame pitcher for the Oakland A's and New York Yankees in the 1970's.

CHAMP. Short for champion.

CHIEF. AFC Kansas City Chiefs football team.

CLIPPER. Los Angeles Clippers, a basketball team (NBA),

COACH. One who trains athletes and athletic teams.

DIZZY DEAN. (1911-1974). Jay Hanna "Dizzy" Dean. Hall of Fame pitcher; sportscaster.

DR. J. Julius Winfield Erving (1950-). Record maker basketball player mostly associated with the New York Nets.

DRIBBLE. In basketball, a dribble is moving the ball along by quick, short bounces.

EIGHT BALL. In the game of pool, the eight ball is black with the number 8 on it.

EXPO. Montreal Expos, a baseball team (NL).

FEATHERWEIGHT. A boxer who weighs between 118 and 127 pounds.

FLO JO. Florence Griffith Joyner (1959-1998). Track and field star and Olympic Gold Medallist.

GOALIE. A goalkeeper assigned to protect the goal in some sports, particularly ice hockey.

GORDIE. Gordie Howe (1928-). Stanley Cup champion ice hockey player. Professional career goals totaled 1071.

GROUNDER. A grounder is when a baseball hits the infield before being caught by the fielder.

HEAD PIN. The head pin or kingpin is the foremost pin in the setup of pins in the game of bowling.

INTIMIDATOR. Dale "The Intimidator" Earnhardt (1951-2001). The first driver killed in the Daytona 500, which began in 1959. He was still a championship contender at age 49.

K-O. A knockout at the end of a boxing match.

KAREEM ABDUL-JABAR. (1947-). Played basketball for the Los Angeles Lakers from 1975-1989. Noted for his "Skyhook," his career high points of 38,387 may never be surpassed.

KNUCKLEBALL. In baseball, type of off-speed ball thrown by the pitcher.

KOBE. Kobe Bryant (1978-). Guard/forward of the Los Angeles Lakers basketball team. Youngest player ever to play in the NBA at 18.

LAKER. Los Angeles Lakers, a basketball team (NBA).

LONGSHOT. An entry in a horse race with only a small chance of winning.

MAGIC. Earvin "Magic" Johnson (1959-). Famed basketball player for the Los Angeles Lakers. His retirement consists of ownership of movie theaters, and a commitment A.I.D.S. education/prevention through the Magic Johnson Foundation.

MICKEY. Mickey Charles Mantle (1931-1995). Beloved Hall of Farmer who played centerfield for the New York Yankees from 1951 to 1968. Broadcaster Bob Costas had eulogized, "He was the most compelling baseball hero of our lifetime."

NADIA. Nadia Comaneci (1961-). Romanian Olympic gold-medalist in gymnastics. At the 1976 Olympics Nadia made history, becoming the first gymnast to ever score a perfect 10.

NIKE. Manufacturer of athletic footwear and apparel.

NORTON. Ken Norton, former heavyweight boxing champion.

PADRE. San Diego Padres, a baseball team (NL).

PELE. World famous soccer star from Brazil.

PENGUIN. Pittsburgh Penguins, a hockey team (NHL).

PIRATE. Pittsburgh Pirates, a baseball team (NL).

POLO. Traditionally an aristocratic sport, played on horseback, believed to have originated in Persia, 2000 B.C.

PUCK. The rubber disk used in ice hockey for scoring.

PUTTER. A short golf club used for putting.

RAIDER. Football team, the Oakland Raiders (1960-1982) moved to Los Angeles (1982-1994), then back to Oakland, until present. They were 3-time Superbowl champs.

RANGER. New York Rangers, a hockey team with the NHL, won the Stanley Cup in 1994. Texas Rangers are a baseball team (AL).

REBOUND. A rebound, in basketball is when the ball bounces off the backboard.

REEBOK. Manufacturer of athletic footwear and apparel.

REGGIE. Reginald Martinez Jackson (1946-). Baseball player with the Oakland A's and New York Yankees. Named "Mr. October" for his World Series prowess.

RIGBY. Cathy Rigby (1952-). Olympic gymnast turned singer/performer.

ROCKET. Roger "The Rocket" Clemens. (1962-). Six-time Cy Young Award winning pitcher with the Boston Red Socks and New York Yankees. His Roger Clemens Foundation is dedicated to helping children.

ROOKIE. A novice player on a team.

RUFFIAN. A fast filly with a brief reigning career in horse racing.

RUGBY. A form of football devised by William Webb Ellis of Rugby College, 1823.

SMARTY JONES. The beleaguered blue-collar Philadelphia colt whose 7-for-7 record makes him the first undefeated winner of the 2004 Kentucky Derby since Seattle Slew in 1977.

SATCHEL. Leroy Robert Paige (1906-1982). Legend of the Negro Leagues, Hall of Fame pitcher inductee 1971, with a baseball career that measured decades: 1926-1950.

SCOUT. The Boys and Girls Scouts (1907; 1909) are international organizations that teach citizenship, survival skills and build character.

SECRETARIAT. (1970-1989). The winner of the 1973 Triple Crown "Big Red" was a much beloved horse. His autopsy revealed the secret to his great love and ability to run: a heart weighing 2 1/2 times the normal size.

SHORTSTOP. The baseball player, whose position is between second and third base.

SHINGO. Shingo Katayama is Japan's fun-loving, flamboyant pro-golfer.

SKI DOG. A skier who spends a lot of time on the slopes.

SLALOM. In downhill skiing, a race down a zigzag course, especially between flags or markers.

SLINGSHOT. Y-shaped primitive weapon with elasticized strap used to fling stones.

SLUGGER. In baseball, a player who gets extra base hits or has a high hitting percentage.

SOX. Boston Red Sox or Chicago White Sox, named for the color the team players wear.

SPARKY. Albert Walker "Sparky" Lyle (1944-). Relief pitcher for the New York Yankees in the 1970's.

SPEEDO. A brand of sportswear swimsuits.

SPINKS. Leon Spinks (1953-). Won a world heavyweight title fight against Muhammad Ali.

SPORT. A game pastime with rules and physical exercise involved.

SPRINT. A short run at maximum speed.

STEELER. Pittsburgh Steelers. Football team in the NFL.

SUMO. A Japanese form of wrestling carried out with traditional ceremony. There are no weight divisions, but there is a system of rank.

SUPERSONIC. Seattle Supersonics, basketball team (NBA).

SURFER. An athlete who catches the crest of a wave on a surfboard and rides it to shore.

TIGER WOODS. (1975-). Eldrick "Tiger" Woods is the youngest, winningest golfer on the professional golfing circuit. With his second Masters victory in 2001, Tiger became the first ever to hold all four professional major championships in one season.

TOUCHDOWN. A play in football that is executed when a player has possession of the ball behind the goal line of the opponent.

TROJAN. University of Southern California Trojans. See "Bruin."

UMPIRE. A person who impartially decides on plays in sports games.

VLADE. Vlade Divac is the 7 ft., 1 in., Yugoslavian basketball player who has played with the L.A. Lakers and Sacramento Kings.

WALLY. Wally Joyner. (1962-). A baseball player, first baseman for the California Angels.

YANKEE. New York Yankees baseball team (AL). They are the winningest team in baseball with 26 World Series titles.

YOGI. Lawrence Peter "Yogi" Berra. (1925-) Hall of Fame baseball player and coach. Also known for his euphemisms such as "It ain't over till it's over" and others, in his 1998 tome "The Yogi Book: 'I Really Didn't Say All That I Said.'"

ZAMBONI. Frank Zamboni (1901-1988). Created the ubiquitous ice-resurfacing machine designed for the use in ice hockey and ice-skating.

CHAPTER 19

FLUFFY PETS

VERY FURRY BEASTS!

Baldy	Fluff-n-Stuff	Godiva	Pooh Bear
Bear; She-Bear	Fluffy	Gorilla	Rapunzel
Beardsley	Foxy	Grizzly	Ruffles
Bushwhacker	Frizzy	Koala	Sasquatch
Bushy	Furball	Ling Ling	Shaggy Dog
Cashmere	Furburger	Marshmallow	Steppenwolf
Chiffon	Furry	Minx	Wolfy
Cottontails	Fuzzball	Mopsey	Woolly
Feathers	Fuzzy	Pom Pom	Yogi Bear

CHAPTER 20

FUNSTERS

FUNNY PETS WITH A
WHIMSICAL NATURE

ABBOTT AND COSTELLO. Bud Abbott (1895-1974). Comic actor who teamed up with vaudevillian Lou Costello (1906-1959). Bud Abbott played straight man to plump partner Lou Costello.

ARSENIO. Arsenio Hall (1955-). Comedian/actor, he was the first African-American to host a successful late night talk show "The Arsenio Hall Show" (1988-1994).

BABA BOOEY. Gary Dell'Abate (1961-). Producer and side kick for radio shock-jock Howard Stern.

BARNUM AND BAILEY. P.T. Barnum (1810-1891). Phineas Taylor Barnum teamed up with James A. Bailey to become "Barnum and Bailey's Ringling Brother's Circus."

BOOSLER, ELAYNE. (1952-). Comedienne/singer/actor/writer is best known for being the first young, unmarried, dressed-up-for-a-date female comedian. Elayne is also a dedicated animal activist.

BUTTONS, RED. (1919-). From burlesque to Broadway and on to Hollywood, Red has had audiences laughing for over 70 years.

CAMPY. An exaggerated, theatrical-like behavior.

CARNEY. A person who works with a carnival.

CARROT TOP. Scott Thompson. Red-headed comedian, known for his trunk-o-tricks.

CARSON. Johnny Carson, was enduring the host of "The Tonight Show" (1962-1992).

CLOWNIE. One who acts in a wacky, zany, campy way.

CURLY. Jerome "Curly" Howard played one of "The Three Stooges" in the mid-1930's.

DING-A-LING. An airhead, or befuddled person, one without a firm grip on reality.

DUBYA. President George W. "Dubya" Bush's (2001-) Texan nickname. One may associate "Dubya" with his comical "Dubya-isms such as, "Rarely is the question asked: 'Is our children learning?'"

FUNNY GIRL. Barbra Streisand (1942-). Singer/actress played Funny Girl, Fanny Brice on Broadway and later in an Academy Award winning performance on film.

FURBY. Furry creatures with a language all their own.

GIDDY. Lightheartedly silly.

HAPPY. Indicating contentment and a good nature.

HIJINKS. Unrestrained fun.

HOKEY. From the word hokum; contrived sentimentality.

IGBY. Igby's was a famous comedy club in Los Angeles.

JESTER. Originally, the comic of the medieval court who entertained royalty.

JOKER. One who tells jokes with punchlines.; a prankster.

KOOKY. An eccentric behavior.

LAMPOON. A written or acted out satire intended to ridicule.

LAUREL AND HARDY. This comedy team was good at slapstick catastrophe. Stan Laurel was the thin and inept counterpart to the portly straight man Oliver Hardy.

LENO. James Douglas Muir "Jay" Leno (1950-). Johnny Carson's successor as host of "The Tonight Show" (1992-). As a stand-up comedian, he is known for being one of the busiest performers in comedy, sometimes booking over 300 appearances annually.

LOONEY TUNES. Warner Brothers' cartoon specials, produced from 1930 to 1933. Characters include Bugs Bunny, Daffy Duck and Elmer Fudd.

MOE. Moses "Moe" Howard (1905-1975). Moe was one of the Three Stooges whose specialty was brute slapstick.

MR. WINKLE. The web-celebrity dog, who is a rescued stray and is the known as "The cutest dog in the universe." His guardian is Lara-Jo Regan.

NIPSEY. Nipsey Russell (1924-). Comedian has made many appearances on T.V., film and on concert stages.

PUNSTER. One who engages in the use of puns or play on words.

QUACKERS. A form of the slang "crackers"; to go mad.

ROBIN. Robin Williams, animated actor/comedian has made memorable appearances on T.V., film and concert stages. See "Mork from Ork."

RONALD MCDONALD. The mascot clown for McDonald's fast-food restaurants.

ROSIE. Rosie O'Donnell. (1962-). Funny lady and star of films, she has added talk-show host and magazine publisher to her repertoire.

SCHIZO. One who acts in a schizophrenic or irrational manner.

SEINFELD. See "T.V."

SHEMP. Samuel "Shemp" Howard (1895-1955). He was one of the Three Stooges.

SINBAD. David Adkins. (1956-). Stand-up comedian/actor got his start on "Star Search."

SMILEY. A person with a perpetual grin.

SPAZ. Shortened form of slang word "spastic" meaning "a bungling person," "a klutz."

STOOGE. A stooge is an entertainer who feeds lines to the main comedian and usually serves as the butt of his jokes.

WACKY. Crazy, outrageous behavior.

YAKOV. Yakov Smirnoff, a comedian from Russia whose tag line was "What a Country!"

ZANY. Acting in a comedic, foolish way.

CHAPTER 21

CATS

OVER 75 NAMES FOR OUR FELINE FRIENDS

Alley Cat	Claws	Garfield	Kitty; Kit
Attack Cat	Cool Cat	Happy Cat	Krazy Kat
Bat Cat	Copy Cat	Hobbes	Le Tigre
Black Cat	Cougar	Ignatz	Leo
Bobcat	Eartha Kitt	Jag	Me-Meow
Boo-Boo Kitty	El Gato	Jaguar	Meowmer
Calico	Fancy Cat	Katarina	Milo
Cat Balou	Fat Cat	Katmandu	Miss Kitty
Catalina	Fellini	Katrina	Morris
Catatonic	Felix	Katzenjammer	Mr. Bigglesworth
Catfish	Figaro	Kit Kat	
Catskills	Fraidy Cat	Kit-n-Kaboodle	Mrs. Whiskerson
Catwoman	Frisky	Kittens	Nine Lives
Cheshire	Fritz	Kitty Hawk	Octopussy

NAME THAT PET!

Panther	Pussy Galore	Sourpuss	Tomcat; Tom Cat
Pink Panther	Pussycat	Stimpy	Top Cat
Puff	Pussywillow	Stray Cat	Whiskers
Puma	Scaredy Cat	Sylvester	
Purr-fect Cat	Scatman	Tabby	
Purry	Snagglepuss	Tiger	
Puss-n-Boots	Snapperpussy	Tigger	

FROM THE MUSICAL "CATS"

Bill Bailey	Electra	Jemima	Rumpus
Admetus	Etcetera	Jennanydots	Rum Tum Tugger
Alonzo	George	Macavity	Rupleteazer
Asparagus	Griddlebone	Mr. Mistoffelees	Sillabub
Bombalurina	Grizabella	Mungojerrie	Skimbleshanks
Bustopher Jones	Growltiger	Munkustrap	Swing
Carbucketty	Gumbie Cat	Old Deuteronomy	Tantomile
Cassandra	Gus the Theatre Cat	Plato	Tumblebrutus
Coricopat	Jellical Cat	Pouncival	Victor; Victoria
Demeter	Jellyorum	Quaxo	

CHAPTER 22

ALPHABETICAL

A

Aahliyah	Aja	Aliyah	Anastacia
Aardvark	Ajax	Ally Gator	Anastasia
Abbey;	Aki	Aloha	Andromeda
Abby	Akua	Alonzo	Andy
Abbot	Alabaster	Alouicious	Angel
Abdul	Aladdin	Alpine	Angus
Abercrombie	Alameda Slim	Alto	Annihilator
Ace	Alamo	Alvin	Animal
Achilles	Alaska	Alzado	Annabus
Admetus	Albie	Amadeus	Annie
Admiral	Albino	Amanda	Ansel
Adolph	Alex	Amazon	Antoine
Aero	Alexis	Ambassador	Apache
Agape	Alfa Romero	Amber	Apeman
Agatha	Alfalfa	Amigo	Aphrodite
Agent Eleven	Alfie	Ammo	Apocalypse
Aibo	Algebra	Amoré	Apollo
Aires	Ali	Amoretto	Apples
	Ali Baba	Amos	Aquarius

Arby	Arsenio	Asta	Auggie Doggie
Archibald	Artemis	Asterix	
Archie	Arthur; Artie	Astin	Auntie Grizelda
Aretha		Astor	Aurora
Arfy	Artoo-Detoo (R2-D2)	Astro	Aussie
Aristotle	Ashes	Athena	Autobahn
Arlo	Ashley	Atlantis	Autumn
Arnold	Asparagus	Atlas	Aztec
Arrow	Aspen	Attila	

B	Baby Doll	Balou; Baloo	Barkley
B.J.	Baby Huey	Bamm Bamm	Barnabas
Baba Booey	Bach	Bambi	Barnaby
Baba Wawa	Backbeat	Bamboozle	Barney
Babalou; (ie)	Bagel	Bananas	Barnum
Babette	Badger	Bandit	Baron
Babe; Baybe	Bagger Vance	Bando	Baroness
Babo	Bailey	Banshee	Barracuda
Babooshka	Baldy	Barbie	Baron
Babs	Bali	Barbarella	Bart
Baby	Balki	Barfly	Bartholomew
Baby Bop	Ballerina	Barkers	Baryshnikov

Bartman	Beemer	Biff	Bitsey
Bashful	Beeno	Big Ben	Bixby
Basil	Beeper	Big Bopper	Black Cat
Batboy	Beethoven	Big Dipper	Blackberry
Batman; Batgirl	Beetle Bailey	Big Foot	Blackhawk
Baxter	Beldar	Big Red	Blackie
Bazooka	Bella; Belle	Bigger	Blackjack
B-Ball	Belle Star	Bee Gee; Bigi; Biji	Blacksmith
Beanie	Benjamin	Bijou	Blackstreet
Bear	Benji	Biko	Blackwell
Beardsley	Benson	Bilbo Baggins	Blaine
Beasley	Bentley	Bilko	Blanco (a)
Beastie Boy	Bernie	Bill Bailey	Blarney
Beatnik	Bert; Burt	Bimbo	Blaze; Blazer
Beau; Bo	Bessie	Binghamton	Blimpie
Beaumont	Betsey	Bingo	Bling Bling
Beauregard	Beulah	Binky	Blintz
Beauty	Bevy	Bionic Dog	Blitz
Beaver	Beyoncé	Birdy	Blondie
Becky	Bianca	Biscuit	Blossom
Beefy	B.B. King; Bibi	Bismarck	Blue; Bleu; Bloo
Beelzebub	Bibs	Bistro	Bluebell

NAME THAT PET!

Bluegrass	Bone Thugs	Boosler	Brigit; Brigitte
Bluto	Bones	Bosco	Brindle
Boa	Bongo	Bosley	Brisney
Bob; Bobby	Bonita	The Boss	Brittany
Boba	Bonkers	Boston	Bro
Bobcat	Bonnie	Boston Beans	Bronco
Bobo	Bono	Bowfinger	Bronson
Bodacious	Bonwitt	Bowie	Brontë
Bodger	Bonzai	Bows	Brooke
Boffo	Bonzo	Bowser	Brown Sugar
Bogart	Boo	Boy	Brownie
Bogg (s)	Boo Boo	Boychek	Brubaker
Bogie	Boo Boo Kitty	Bozo	Bruce
Bogus	Boog	Brady	Bruin
Boink	Boogie	Brahms	Bruiser
Bojangles	Booker	Brando	Bruno
Bomber	Booker T	Brandon	Brutus
Boomerang	Boom Boom	Brandy	Bubba
Bon Bon	Boomer	Bravo	Bubbles
Bon Jovi	Boone	Bree; Brie	Bubele
Bond, James Bond	Booth	Breezy	Buck
Bonehead	Boots	Brewski	Buckaroo
		Brewster	

Bucko | Bugeye | Bumper | Butch

Buckshot | Bugle Boy | Bundy | Butkus

Buckwheat | Buggs | Bungee | Butterfingers

Bucky | Bugsy | Bunko | Buttercup

Bud; Buddy | Bull's Eye | Bunny | Butterfly

Buddha | Bull (y) | Burrito | Buttons

Buddy | Bulfinch | Busby | Buzz Lightyear

Buford | Bullet | Bush (y) | Buzzsaw

Buffalo Bill | Bullethead | Bushwhacker | Byron

Buffy | Bullwinkle | Buster

C

C.B. | Calico | Cappuccino | Carmel

C.D. | Caligula | Cappy | Carnie (ey)

C.J. | Calliope | Caprice | Carob

Caboose | Calvin | Captain | Carrot Top

Cadpig | Calypso | Captain Ahab | Carson

Caesar | Camelot | Captain Bly | Carvel

Cagney | Campy | Captain Kangaroo | Casey; K.C.

Cajun | Cana; Kana | Captain Kirk | Cashmere

Calamity Jane | Candy | Captain Nemo | Casper

Cali | Caneska | Carafe | Casanova

| Cannon | Carbucketty | Cassidy

Cassie	Chaplin	Cher	Chipmunk
Cat Balou	Charcoal	Cherie	Chiquita
Cat-o-Nine Tails	Chardonnay	Cherish	Chivas
	Charisma	Cherokee	Chong
Catastrophe	Charity	Cherry	Choo Choo
Catatonic	Charlemagne	Cheshire	Chopin
Catfish	Charles; Charlie (ey)	Chester	Chopstix
Cavier		Chestnut	Chubby
Cayenne	Charm	Chewbacca	Chuckles
Cecil	Charo	Chewy	Chucky
Chablis	Chartreuse	Chex	Churchill
Chachi	Chase	Cheyenne	Chutney
Chainsaw	Chassie	Chia Pet	Chynna
Cha Cha	Chastity	Chickie	Ciji
Chaka	Chatterbox	Chico (a)	Cinder
Chalet	Chaucer	Chief	Cinderella
Chamois	Chauncey	Chiffon	Cinnamon
Champ; Champion	Chaz	Chili	Cisco
Champagne	Checkers	Chilly Willy	Clancey
Chan	Cheddar	Chin Chin	Clarence
Chanel	Cheech	Chinook	Clark Kent
Chap (s)	Cheesecake	Chip; Chipper	Claude
	Chelsea		

ALPHABETICAL

Claudius	Columbus	Cornelius	Crimson
Claws	Comanche	Cornflake	Critter
Clay	Comet	Corona	Cruella De Vil
Clementine	Commander	Cory	
Cleo	Commando	Cosby	Crusader Rabbit
Cleopatra	Comrade	Cosmic	Crystal
Clifford	Conan	Cosmo	Cubby
Clipper	Conehead	Costello	Cuddles
Cloe; Chloe	Confucius	Cotton Tail	Cujo
Clover	Conga	Couch Potato	Cupcake
Clownie	Conquistador	Count; Countess	Cupid
Clumsy Carp	Contessa		Curlicue
Coach	Convict	Courage	Curly
Coal	Coochie-Coo	Cowabunga	Curry
Cobra	Cookie	Cowboy; Cowgirl	Custer
Coco; Cocoa; Koko	Cool Cat	Crackerjack	Cutter
Cody	Cool Dog	Crackers	Cyborg
Cognac	Cooley	Cranberry	Cyclops
Colby	Cooper	Crash	Cyrano
Colonel	Copperfield	Cream Puff	Cyrus
Colonel Klink	Coricopat	Crewcut	Czar; Czarina
Columbo	Corky	Cricket	

D

D.C.

D.D.; Didi;
Dee Dee

D.J.

D.J. Jazzy Jeff

D.O.G.

Dabney

Dagwood

Dahlia

Daiquiri

Daisy

Dakota

Dalai Lama

Damien

Dana

Dancer

Dandy

Dante

Daphne

Dapper Dog

Darby

Darkman

Darla

Darth Vadar

Dash

Data

Dawg

Deacon

Deitrich

Delilah

Demi

Demitri (ia)

Demon

Denzel

Deputy Dawg

Desi

Destiny

Deter

Devil Dog

Devo

Devon

Dewey

Dex; Dexter

Di

Diablo

Diamond

Dibs

Dickens

Dickie

Diddley

Dido

Diefenbaker

Digby

Digger

Digit

Dijon

Dillinger

Dilly

Dimples

Dinah

Ding Dong

Ding-a-ling

Dingbat

Dingo

Dino

Dion

Dippy Dog

Disco Dog

Disney

Ditto

Ditzi

Diva

Divot

Dixie

Dizzy

Dobber

Dobie Gillis

Doberwoman

Dobie Dog

Doc

Dodie

Dog-a-Muffin

Dogberry

Doggie;
Doggie Daddy

Dogmatic

Dolce

Dolly

Dolomite

Domino

Dondi

Donatello

Donovan

Doobie

Doodles

Doogie Bowser

Doogie Howser

Dooley

Doonesbury

DOS

Dots; Dottie

Doughboy

Doxie

Dr. Doolittle

Dr. Dre

Dr. J.

Dr. Jekyl

Dr. Kildare

Dr. Watson

Drabble

Dragon

Drake

Drexel

Dreyfuss

Dribble

Drizella

Droopy

Druid

Dubya

Duchess

Duckey

Dude; Dudette

Dudley Do Right

Duffy

Duke

Dumbo

Duster

Dusty

Dutch

Dwayne

Dweezil

Dybbuk

Dylan

Dynamo

E

E.T.

E.Z. Dog

Eagle Eye

Eaglehurst Gilette

Earl

Eartha Kitt

Ebineezer

Ebony

Echo

Edgar

Edison

Ego

Eight Ball

Einstein

Eldin

Electra

Elf

Elijah

Elmer Fudd

Elmo

Eloise

Elroy

Elsa

Elsie

El-Train

Elvez

Elvira

Elvis

Elwood

Eminem

Emma

Emmet

Emperor

Empress

Englebert

Enoch

Enos

Ensign

NAME THAT PET!

Eraserhead	Etcetera	Eunice	Excalibur
Ernie	Ethel	Europa	Expo
Eros	Etsel	Evel Knievel	Ezekiel
Escrow	Eubie	Ewok	Ezra

F

Fabian	Fearless	Fidget	Flipper
Fabergé	Feathers	Fido (a)	Flo Jo
Faith	Feisty	Fiesta	Floppy
Faithful	Feivel Mousekewitz	Fifi	Flopsey
Fala	Felicity	Figaro	Floyd
Falafel	Feliz	Figi (j)	Flubber
Fancy Cat	Fella; Feller	Filmore	Fluffy
Fang	Fellini	Filo	Flush
Fanny	Femme	Finian	Flygirl
Fantasia	Feng Shui	Fire	Fonzie
Farfel	Ferdinand	Flame	Forester
Fat Cat	Fergie	Flash	Four Paws
Fatso	Fernando	Flaxen	Foxy; Foxy Lady
Fauna	Ferrari	Flea	Frack
Faux Pas	Ferris Bueller	Fleabag	Fraidy Cat
Fawn	Fester	Fletch	Frank-n-Further
Fax	Festus	Flim Flam Man	Frankenstein
		Flip	

Frankenweenie	Freedom	Frisky (ee)	Fulkner
Frankie	Freejack	Frito Bandito	Funny Face
Franz	Freeway	Fritz	Funny Girl
Fraulein	Frenchy	Frizzy	Funnybone
Frazier	Fresca	Frodo	Furball
Freckles	Fresh Prince	Froggy	Furburger
Fred	Fresno	Frosty	Furby
Freddy Kruger	Frick	Fu Manchu	Furry
Frederick	Friday	Fu-Fu	Fury
Freebie	Frigate	Fudge	Fuzzball
Freebo	Frisco	Fugee	Fuzzy

G

G.I. Joe	Garp	Genius	Giddy
Gabby	Garth	Gentle Ben	Gideon
Gabrielle	Gato	George	Gidget
Galileo	Gator	Georgie Porgie	Gigantor
Gallagher	Gatsby	Georgio	Giggles
Gandalf	Gaylord	Geraldo	Gigi
Gandhi	Geezer	Geronimo	Gigolo
Garbo	Gekko	Gertie; Gertrude	Gilda
Garfield	Gemini	Geselle	Gilley
Gargantua	General	Gibson	Gilligan
	Genghis Khan		Gilmore

NAME THAT PET!

Gilroy	Golda	Gordo	Groupie
Gimlet	Goldfinger	Gorilla	Grover
Gimpy	Goldie	Governor	Grumpy
Ginger	Goldilocks	Grady	Gucci
Ginzu	Goliath	Granny	Guido
Girly	Gomer Pyle	Granuaile	Guiness
Gizmo	Gomez	Gremlin	Gumbel
Gladiator	Gonif	Gretchen	Gumbo
Glastnost	Gonzo	Gretel	Gumby
Glen	Goober	Greta	Gummi Bear
Gnarly	Goochie	Greystoke	Gummo
Gnome	Good Burger	Griffin	Gumshoe
Goalie	Goodfella	Grinch	Gunnar
Goblin	Goofy	Griswald	Guru
Godfrey	Goonie	Grizzly	Gus
Godiva	Gopher	Grog	Guy
Godunov	Gorby	Groover	Gypsy
Godzilla	Gordie (y)	Groucho	

H	Halavah	Halle; (ie)	Hamilton
Hadley	Hale-Bopp	Halo	Hamlet
Hagar	Haley	Hamantashen	Hammer
Haiku	Half-pint	Hambone	Handsome

Hank

Hannah

Hannibal the Cannibal

Hans (z)

Hanzel

Happy

Happy Cat

Hardy

Harley

Harlow

Harmony

Harpo

Harriet

Harry Potter

Harvey

Hat Trick

Hawk

Hawkeye

Hazel

Head Pin

Heathcliff

Heather

Heavy D.

Heckle; Heckles

Heide

Heinekin

Helga

Helios

Helmut

Hemingway

Henry; Henrietta

Her

Herbie

Hercule Poirot

Hercules

Herman

Hermes

Hero

Hershey

Hibachi

Hickory

Hidalgo

Higgins

Highlander

Hijinks (x)

Hilda

Hillbilly

Him

Hip Hop

Hitchcock

Hobbes

Hobbit

Hobo

Hogan

Hogie

Hokey

Holly

Homeboy; Homegirl

Homer Pigeon

Homey the Clown

Honey

Honeybee

Honeydew

Honeysuckle

Honua

Hook

Hooligan

Hooper

Hoosier

Hooch

Hoover

Hopalong Cassidy

Hope

Hopi

Hopper

Horatio

Horshack

Hoser

Hoss

Hot Dog

Hotrod

Houdini

Houlihan

Hound Dog

Howdy Doody

NAME THAT PET!

Hubcap Huffington Humphrey Hutch

Huckleberry Hound Huggy Bear Humvee

Hulk Hogan Hunter

Hud Hummel Hush Puppy

I

I-Ching

Ice

Ice Cream

Ice Cube

Ice T

Ichabod

Icicle

Ickey

Igby

Iggy India Isuzu

Igloo Indiana Jones Itchy

Ignatz Indigo Itsy Bitsy

Ignatius Indy Itty Bit

Ignatowski Ingrid Ivan Ho

Igor Injun Ivan the Terrible

Ike Inspector Ivana

Imelda Intimidator Ivory

Inch Ipo Izod

Index Irving Izzy

J

J.C.; Jay Cee

J.D.

J.J.

J. Lo

J.R.

J.T. Jake Java

Jack Jam Jaws

Jack Frost Jambalaya Jax

Jackson Jammer Jazz

Jacque Jasmine Jazzman

Jaggar Jason Jeannie

Jaguar; Jag Jasper Jeckle

Jed	Jezebel	Johnny	Juggernaut
Jedi	Jiffy Pop	Joker	Jughead
Jeepers	Jigsaw	Jolly	Jugs
Jeff	Jill	Joplin	Juice
Jelly Belly	Jiminy Cricket	Jordan	Julius
Jellybean	Jiminy Glick	Josie	Juliette
Jellyroll	Jingles	Jowls	Jumbo
Jerry	Jingo	Jox	Jumper
Jessie	Jinx	Joy	Junior
Jester	Jip	Ju Ju	Juniper
Jet	Jo Jo	Jubilee	Juno; Juneau
Jethro	Jocko	Jude	Jupiter
Jetson	Jody (i)	Judge	Justice
Jetta	Joe Friendly	Judo	Justy
Jewel	John Doe	Judy	

K	Kafka	Kanani	Katie (y)
K.B.; Kay Bee	Kahlúa	Kanook	Katzenjammer
K.C.; Casey	Kahuna	Kareem	Katmandu
K.D.	Kaiser	Karma	Katrina
Kablam	Kaleidoscope	Kasha	Kayla
Kabuki	Kamikaze	Katarina	Kazam

Kazoo	Khaki	Kirby	Kojak
Keanu	Kibitzer	Kismet	Kokomo
Keely	Kid	Kit Kat	Kona
Keema; Kima (o)	Kieka	Kittens	Kong
Keeper	Kielbasa	Kitty; Kit	Kookaburra
Keesha; Kiesha	Kiki	Kiwi	Kooky
	Killer	Klinger	Kool Moe Dee
Kel	Kimba	Klingon	Kopy Kat
Kelbo	Kimmie	Klondike	Kotch
Kelly	Kimono	Klutz	Krazy Kat
Kelsey	King	Knick Knack	Kreskin
Kelso	Kingfish	Knicker-bocker	Krishna
Kemosabe	Kingpin	Knuckleball	Kubiak
Ken; Kenny	King Timahoe	Knucklehead	Kukla
Kenan	King Tut	Koala	Kuma
Keno	Kinky	Kobe	Kunta Kinte
Kermit	Kip	Kodiak	Kyoto

L

LL Cool J	Lacy	Laika	Lampoon
La Bamba	Laddie Boy	Lainie	Lancelot
	Lady	Lallapalooza	Lani
	Ladybug	Lamb Chop	Lariat Pete

ALPHABETICAL

Lariat Sam	Leonardo	Linus	Lolita
Larou	Leprechaun	Lionel	Lollipop
Lars	Leroy Brown	Lira	Lone Ranger
Larz	Lexis	Little Big Man	Loner
Lassie	Libby	Little Boy Blue	Long Fellow
Latté	Liberace	Little Bunny Foo Foo	Longshot
Laurel	Liberty	Little Dipper	Lonnie; Loni
Layla	Libra	Little Girl	Lookie-Loo
Lazar	Licorice	Little Man Tate	Looney Tunes
Lazarus	Lido	Little Orphan Annie	Lost Boy; Girl
Lazlo	Liebchen	Liza	Lottie
Lazy Dog	Lieutenant	Lizzy	Lotto
Le Pup	Lightfoot	Llewellyn	Lotus
Le Tigre	Lil' Abner	Lobi	Louie
Leader	Lil' Bit	Lobo	Loupgarou
Leatherface	Lil' Guy	Loch Ness	Lovey
Leeloo	Lil' Miss Muffet	Loco Perro	Luana
Left Eye	Lilac	Lodi	Lucas
Lefty	Lilly	Logan	Lucifer
Legs	Lima	Lojack	Lucky
Lenny	Limo	Loki	Lucy
Leno	Ling Ling	Lola	Ludwig
Leo			Luger

Lughead	Lula	Lummox	Lupe
Luigi	Lullaby	Lumpy	Lurch
Luke Skywalker	Lulu	Luna	Luther

M

MG	Magnet	Mambo	Marley
Mac	Magnolia	Mammoth	Marlow
Macaroni	Magnum	Mammy	Marmaduke
MacGyver	Magpie	Mandy	Marshmallow
Macgreggor	Mah Jong	Manfred	Marvel
Machine Gun	Mahogany	Mangy	Marvin Martian
Macho	Mai Tai	Maniac	Marz
Macy	Maid Marian	Mannix	Master
Mad Dog	Maimie	Mantra	Matador
Madame Bovary	Mainframe	Manu	Maude
Maddie	Maisie	Mao	Maui
Mademoiselle	Majesty	Marbles	Maven
Madonna	Major	Mardi Gras	Maverick
Magenta	Makamaka	Margarita	Max; Maxine
Maggie	Makani	Mariah	Max Headroom
Magic	Malcom X	Maribelle	Maxi
Magilla Gorilla	Mama Cass	Mario	Maximillian

Maxwell Smart

May May

Maynard G. Krebbs

Mayo

Mayor

Mazel

McCloud

McDuff

McGruff

McMurphy

Meathead

Medea

Megan

Mei Xiang

Mel; Melvin

Melba

Melrose

Memo

Mensa

Mensch

Mercedes

Merci

Mercury

Mercy

Merlin

Mermaid

Merry (i)

Mescal

Meshugge

Metallica

Mew Mew

Mia

Michelangelo

Mickie D.

Mickey Mouse

Midas

Midget

Midnight

Mighty Dog

Mike

Mikey

Miko

Miles

Millie

Milo

Milton

Mimi; Me Me; Mee Mee

Mindy

Ming

Mini; Minnie

Mini Me

Mink Deville

Minky

Minerva

Minx

Miracle

Mirage

Miranda

Mischief

Misfit

Mishka

Miss Brooks

Miss Kitty

Miss Moneypenny

Missy

Mister Ed

Mister Man

Mistress

Misty

Mittens

Mitzvah

Mitzi

Mix

Miyagi

Mo Mo

Moby

Moby Dick

Mocha

Moe

Moesha

Mohammad

Mojo

Molasses

Molly

Mona Lisa

Mondo

Monique

Monkeybone

Monroe; Munro

NAME THAT PET!

Monsieur

Monster

Montgomery

Monty Python

Moocher

Moody

Mookie

Moon; Moon Unit

Moonbaby

Moonbeam

Moondoggie

Moonwalker

Moose

Moppet

Mopsey

Mordecai

Morgan

Mork from Ork

Morris

Morticia

Mortimer Snerd

Moses

Motley

Motor Mouth

Mouser

Moxie

Mozart

Mr. Bean

Mr. Big

Mr. Bigglesworth

Mr. Biggs

Mr. Boffo

Mr. Bojangles

Mr. Chips

Mr. Dithers

Mr. Freeze

Mr. Green Jeans

Mr. Hyde

Mr. Magoo

Mr. Moose

Mr. Mister

Mr. Peebles

Mr. Peepers

Mr. Potato Head

Mr. Pugsley

Mr. Rogers

Mr. Snuffleupagus

Mr. T

Mr. Tibbs

Mr. Winkle

Mrs. Claus

Mrs. Whiskerson

Ms. Musso

Ms. Piggy

Mu-Gu

Muchacha (o)

Muddy Waters

Mudwhomper

Muffin

Muffy

Muggles

Mugs

Mugsey

Mugwump

Mummanshantz

Mummy

Munchie

Munchkin

Munster

Muppet

Murdock

Murphy

Murray

Muscles

Mush

Muskrat

Musketeer

Mussolini

Mutley

Mutt

N

99

Nadia

Nakita

Nanook

Napoléon

Nappy

Nasty Dog

Natasha

Naughty Dog

Neanderthal

Nebula

Needles

Negra

Negrita

Nell (ie; y)

Nelson

Nemesis

Nemo

Neptune

Nero

Newton

Nibbles

Nickelodeon

Nicodemus

Nietzsche

Nigel

Nijinsky

Nike

Nikki (y)

Nimble

Nimbu

Nimitz

Nine Lives

Ninja

Niña (o)

Nimo

Nipper

Nipsey

Nirvana

Nixon

No Name

Noche

Nomad

Nome (i)

Noodles

Nook

Noonie

Norm;
Norman

Norton

Nosh

Nostradamus

Nouba

Nova

Nudnik

Nudgh

Nugget

Nuke Laloosh

Nureyev

Nutmeg

O

Oaf

Obi-Wan
Kenobi

Obo; Oboe

Octopussy

Oddball

Odessa

Odie

Officer
Krupke

Offissa Pup

Oggie

Oingo Boingo

Oki

Oksana

Old King Cole

Old Yeller

Olga

Olive;
Olive Oyl

Oliver; Ollie

Olivia

Olympia

Omar	Opie	Orville	Otto
Omega	Orbit	Oscar	Ouija; Weejie
Onyx	Orchid	Osgood	Outlaw
Oodles	Oreo	Osh Kosh	Ouzi
Oompah	Orion	Oso	Oz
Opal	Orka	Othello	Ozwald
Ophelia	Orphan	Otis	Ozzie

P	Paloma	Patches	Pearl
P-C	Panama	Patience	Pebbles
P. Diddy	Pancho	Patrick	Pedro
P.J.	Panda	Patriot	Pee Wee; P-Oui
Pablo	Pandora	Patsy	Peebo
Pac Man	Panther	Patti Cake	Pegleg
Pace	Papaya	Paul Pry	Peppers
Pacer	Pappy	Pavarotti	Pegasus
Paco	Parfait	Pavlov	Pele
Paddington Bear	Party Girl; Boy	Paws	Pembroke
Paddy	Pasha	Pea Pod	Penguin
Pago	Passion	Peabody	Penny; Penelope
Paisano	Pasta	Peaches	
Pal	Pat	Peanut	Pepe Le Pew

Pepper	Phoebe	Pippin	Pompeii
Peppy	Phoenix	Pipsqueak	Ponce
Pepsi	Picasso	Pirate	Ponch
Pepto	Piccadilly	Pisces	Pongo
Perci (y)	Piccolo	Pistachio	Pontius Pilot
Perdita	Pickles	Pistol Pete	Pony Boy
Periwinkle	Pico	Pita	Pooch; Poochie
Perro	Piddles	Pixie	
Peso	Pie Face	Plato	Poochini, Puccini
Pesto	Pierre	Pluto	Pooh Bah
Pet	Piffle	Po	Pooh Bear
Pete	Piglet	Pockets	Pookie
Peter Pan	Pigpen	Poco	Poopsey
Petey	Pigtail	Pogo	Popeye
Petite	Pinball	Poindexter	Poppy
Petra	Ping	Pointer	Porche
Petula	Pinhead	Poison	Popsicle
Petunia	Pinky	Pokemon	Poptart
Peugeot	Pinnochio	Pokey	Poquito
Pez	Pita	Polynesia	Porgy
Phantom	Piper	Polly	
Pharaoh	Pippi Longstocking	Polo	Porkchop
Phineas		Pom Pom	Porky

NAME THAT PET!

Porter	Princess Di	Puff (y)	Puppers
Poser	Princessa	Puff Daddy	Puppet
Posh	Priscilla	Pufnstuf	Puppy
Potpourri	Pristina	Pugsley	Purr-fect Cat
Pouncival	Professor	Puli	Pushinka
Precious	Professor Marvel	Puma	Puss-n-Boots
Preppie	Prudence	Pumpkin	Pussy Cat
President; Prez	Prymaat	Pundit	Pussy Galore
Presto	Psyche	Punim	Pussywillow
Pretzel	Pua	Punkin	Putter
Primadonna	Puck	Punky	Putty
Primo	Puddin'	Punster	Puzzles
Prince	Puddles	Punxsutawney Phil	Pygmalion
Princess	Pudgy	Pup	Pygmy
			Python

Q

Quackers	Quartermaine	Queen Latifah	Quimby
Quark	Quasimoto	Queenie	Quincy
	Quaxo	Quigley	Quinn

R

Radical "Rad" Dog

Raffy

Raggedy Ann; Andy

Rags

Rain

Rainbow

Ralph

Rambler

Rambo

Ranger

Raphael

Rapper

Rapunzel

Rascal

Rasputin

Rasta Man

Ratdog

Ratso Rizzo

Raven

Razzie

Razzmatazz

Reanimator

Reba

Rebel

Reebok

Rebound

Recycle

Red

Red Devil

Reflex

Reggae

Reggie; Reginald

Remington Steele

Remo

Ren

Renegade

Replay

Rerun

Retro

Revolver

Rex

Rhett

Rhiannon

Rhubarb

Ribbit

Ricky

Ricochet

Riley

Rin Tin Tin

Ringo

Rio

Rip

Ripley

Ritz

Rob Roy

Robin

Robin Hood

Robo Dog

Rochester

The Rock

Rockefeller

Rocket

Rocket Man

Rocko

Rockwell

Rocky

Roger

Rojo

Roker

Romeo

Rommel

Romper

Ronald McDonald

Roosevelt

Roper

Rory

Rosarita

Roscoe

Rose; Rosie

Rosebud

Rottenweiler

Rouge

Roulette

Rover

Rowdy

Roxanne	Rudy; Rudolph	Rufus	Runt
Roxette		Rugby	Rusty
Roxie	Rue	Rugula	Rutger
Royal	Ruff	Rumblefish	
Ruble	Ruffian	Rumplestiltskin	
Ruby	Ruffles	Runner	

S

Sable	Samantha	Satin	Schroeder
Sabre	Sambo	Saturn	Scooby-Doo
Sabrina	Sammo	Savannah	Scooter
Sacajewea	Samson	Sawdust	Scorpio
Sadie	Sandy	Saxon; Saxony	Scorpion King
Saffy	Santa	Scamp	Scottie; Scotto
Sage	Sapphire	Scarecrow	Scoundrel
Sailor Boy	Sarah	Scaredy Cat	Scout
Saint	Sasha	Scarface	Scrapper
Saki	Sashi	Scarlet	Scraps
Salem	Sasquatch	Scatman	Screech
Salsa	Sassafras	Scavenger	Scruff (y)
Salty Dog	Sassy	Schatzie	Scuba
Sam	Satan	Schitzo	Searcher
Sammy	Satchel	Schnapps	Sebastian
	Satchmo	Schooner	Secretariat

See Saw	Shazam!	Shuggie	Siren
Seinfeld	She-Bear	Shuggims	Sisqo
Senator	Sheba	Shultz	Sissy
Sequoia	Sheena	Sid the Sloth	Six
Sergeant	Sheik	Siddhartha	Sizzle
Shadow	Shelby	Sidekick	Skeet; Skeeter
Shady	Shemp	Sidewinder	Skeezix
Shaggy	Shep	Sidney; Sydney	Skidog
Shakespeare	Sherlock Holmes		B.F. Skinner
Shaky		Sienna	Skip; Skippy; Skipper
Shalimar	Sherman	Sierra	
Shalom	Sherwood	Siesta	Skittles
Shamrock	Shiksa	Sigmund	Skye
Shamsky	Shilo	Sigourney	Slam
Shamu	Shiny	Sillabub	Slappy
Shamus	Shingo	Silver	Slash
Shana	Shmutz	Silverado	Slater
Shane	Shogun	Simka	Sledgehammer
Shannon	Short Stop	Simon	Sleepy
Shark; Sharkey	Shorty	Sinbad	Slick
Shasta	Shoshone	Sioux	Slim
Shaynie	Shrek	Sir Lancelot	Slim Shady
	Shrimp	Sir Philip	Slinky

NAME THAT PET!

Slippers	Whiplash	Solo	Spike
Slugger	Sniffler	Solomon	Spinks
Sluggo	Sniffles	Somba	Spin; Spinner
Slush Puppy	Snookers	Sonnet	Spirit
Smarty Jones	Snooky	Sonny Boy	Spiro
Smedley	Snoopy	Sounder	Splash
Smidgen	Snow White	Sourpuss	Spock
Smidget	Snowball	Spacey	Spook
Smiley	Snowflake	Spade	Sport (y)
Smitty	Snowy	Spanky	Spot; Spots
Smokey	Snubby	Sparky	Spotless
Smoochy	Snuffy	Sparkle	Spotto
Smudge	Snuggles	Spartacus	Spotty
Smurf	Sock Puppet	Spartan	Spring
Snagglepuss	Socks; Sox	Spaz	Sprinkles
Snake	Socrates	Speckles	Sprint
Snapper	Soda Pop	Speedo	Sprout
Snapperpussy	Sofie; Sophia	Speedy Gonzales	Spuds
Snappy	Soho	Spencer	Spunky
Sneakers	Soldier	Sphinx	Sputnik
Sneaky	Soleil	Spice Girl	Squaw
Snickers	Solitaire	Spicy	Squeak (y)
Snidely	Solly		Squeeze

Squiggly	Stoli	Sulley	Suzuki
Squiggy	Stomper	Sultan	Swami
Squint	Stooge	Summer	Swayze
Squire	Stormy	Sumo	Sweathog
Squirt	Stranger	Sunbeam	Sweeny
Stanley	Stray Cat	Sunburst	Sweet Pea
Stardust	Streaker	Sundance	Sweetheart
Star	Striper;	Sunny (i)	Sweetie
Starlet	Stripes	Sunrise	Sweetlips
Starsky	Stuart Little	Sunset	Sweetie Pie
Steeler	Stubby	Sunshine	Swifty
Steppenwolf	Stumpy	Sunspot	Swing (er)
Stick	Stymie	Super Dog	Swisher
Sting	Styx	Supersonic	Swoozie
Stinker	Subaru	Surfer	Sybil
Stinky	Sugar	Survivor	
Stitch	Sugar Bear	Sushi	
Stogey	Suki	Suzie Q	

T	T.J.	Taco	Tammy (i)
T-Bone	Tabby	Tadpole	Tana
T-Boz	Tabitha	Taffy	Tandy
T.C.	Taca	Taj	Tang

NAME THAT PET!

Tangerine	Tuxedo	Tiffany	Toby
Tango	Tenga	Tiger	Toehead
Tank	Tengu	Tiger Woods	Toffee
Tantomile	Tequila	Tigger	Tofu
Tanya	Terminator	Tiki	Toga
Tar Baby	Tess; Tessa; Tessie	Tillie	Togo
Tara		Timber	Tom
Tartuffe	Texas	Tin Man	Tom Cat
Tarzan	Thatcher	Tinkerbell	Tom Thumb
Tasha	Thelma	Tino; Tina	Toma
Taster	Thelonious	Tiny	Tomboy
Tattoo	Theo; Theodore	Tiny Tim	Tommy (i)
Tatters	Thin Man	Tip-Toe	Tonga
Taurus	Thor	Tippi	Tonka
Tawny	Thoreau	Tipler	Tonto
Taxi	Thumbelina	Tipsey	Toodles
Taz; Tazmanian Devil	Thumper	Tish (a)	Tootie
Teacup	Thunderbolt	Titan	Tootsie; Tootsie Roll
Teddy (i)	Thunderheart	Titanic	Topaz
Teeny Weenie	Tian Tian	Tito	Top Cat
Tempo	Tic-Tac	Titus	Topo Gigio
Tennessee	Tidbit	Tizzy	Topper

Topsider	Trapper John	Trooper	Tupper
Topsie	Trekkie	Trouble	Turbo
Tornado	Triffle	Trucker	Turdley
Tor; Tora; Toro	Trigger	Trudy (i)	Tux
	Trifle	Truffles	Tweedle Dee
Totellini	Trinket	Truman	Tweedle Dum
Tosh	Tripod	Tsunami	Tweety Bird
Totem	Tripper	Tu-Tu	Twiggy
Toto	Trivia	Tubbs	Twinkie
Touchdown	Trixie	Tucker	Twinkle
Toy Toy	Troika	Tuffy	Twinkle Toes Flintstone
Tram	Trojan	Tulip	
Tramp	Troll	Tumbleweed	Ty; Tai
Transformer	Trolley	Tumblebrutus	Tyler
Trapper	Tron	Tundra	Tyrone

U

	Ulysses	Uncle Sam	Urkel
Ubu	Ump; Umpire	Underdog	Ursula
Uggie	Uncle Miltie	Undertaker	Utopia

V

	Valentino	Van Gogh	Vanity
Vagabond	Vampire	Vanilla	Vegas
Valentine	Vampirella	Vanilla Ice	Velcro

NAME THAT PET!

Velvet	Victory	Virgo	Vladimir
Venus	Villa	Viscount	Vogue
Vesta	Violet	Vixen	Voltaire
Vette	Viper	Vlade	Vulcan

W

Wacky	Weasel	Whiskey	Willy Wonka
Wafer	Webster	White Fang	Wilma
Waggin' Tails	Wednesday	White Tips	Wimpy
Wags	Wee Willie Winkie	Whitey	Wind; Windy
Waif	Weebo	Whitley	Windsong
Waldo	Weedwhacker	Whitney	Wink (s); Winky
Wally	Weejie	Whoopie (ee)	Winnie the Pooh
Walrus Chumley	Weenie	Widget	Winston
Wampum	Weezer; Wheezer	Wiffle	Winthrop
Wanda	Wench	Wiggins	Wishbone
Warden	Wendy	Wiggles	Wiz; Wizard
Warrior	Wentworth	Wigwam	Wizzo
Watchdog	Whammy	Wilhemina	Wolf
Watson	Wheatie	Wilbur	Wolfgang
Waylon	Wheaton	Wiley, Wil-E-Coyote	Wolfy
Wayne	Whiplash	Willard; Willie	Wonder Dog
	Whiskers	Willow	

Woodrow

Woodstock

Woody
Chew Shoes

Wooky

Wooley

Wrinkles

X

X-ray

Xavier

Xena

Xeno

Xenon

Xu Xa

Y

Yakov

Yang

Yankee

Yanni

Yenta

Yentl

Yeoman

Yin

Yo Yo

Yo-Yo Ma

Yoda

Yogi Bear

Yoki

Yoko

Yosemite Sam

Yoshi

Young MC

Yowser

Yucca

Yuki

Yukon

Yuppie Dog

Yutz

Z

Zack; Zak

Zamboni

Zany

Zap

Zappa

Zappy

Zelda

Zelli

Zen

Zenith

Zephyr

Zero

Zeus

Zigfield

Zigfried

Ziggy

Zigzag

Zima

Zing;
Zinger

Zippy

Zodiak

Zoe

Zoltar

Zombie

Zooey

Zooky

Zorba

Zorro

Zowie

Zsa Zsa

Zuki

Zulu

Zuni

Zydeco

INDEX

NAME THAT PET!

INDEX

INDEX

NAME THAT PET!

INDEX

NAME THAT PET!

INDEX

We hoped you enjoyed this book and would
appreciate your feedback.

Feel free to send us your comments to:

Cousin Alice's Press
P.O. Box 5008
Sherman Oaks, CA 91403

Have we missed any names you might recommend
for another volume?

_____

_____

_____

_____

To order additional copies:
Please send check or money order
in the amount of $12.99 USD
(CA residents add 8.25% sales tax)
plus $2.95 shipping and handling to:

Cousin Alice's Press
P.O. Box 5008
Sherman Oaks, CA 91403
USA

or:

www.amazon.com
www.CousinAlicesPress.com